To:

_____

From:

_____

Date:

_____

You're one Cool Guy

Carolyn Larsen

CHRISTIAN ART PUBLISHERS

Published by Christian Art Publishers
PO Box 1599, Vereeniging, 1930, RSA

© 2009
First LuxLeather edition 2015

Text copyright © 2009 by Educational Publishing Concepts.
All rights reserved.

Designed by Christian Art Publishers

Images used under license from Shutterstock.com

Scripture quotations are taken from the *Holy Bible*, New Century Version®.
Copyright © 1987, 1988, 1991, 2005 by Word Publishing, a division of
Thomas Nelson, Inc. Used by permission.

Scripture quotations are taken from the *Holy Bible*, New International Version® NIV®.
Copyright © 1973, 1978, 1984 by International Bible Society. Used by permission
of Zondervan Publishing House. All rights reserved.

Scripture quotations are taken from the *Holy Bible*, New Living Translation®,
second edition. Copyright © 1996, 2004 by Tyndale House Publishers, Inc.,
Carol Stream, Illinois 60188. All rights reserved.

Scripture quotations are taken from the *Holy Bible*, Contemporary English Version®.
Copyright © 1995 by American Bible Society. All rights reserved.

Set in 12 on 14 pt Palatino LT Std by Christian Art Publishers

Printed in China

ISBN 978-1-4321-2311-6

19   20   21   22   23   24   25   26   27   28   –   19   18   17   16   15   14   13   12   11   10

Printed in Shenzhen, China
February 2019
Print Run: 100464

Foreword

How do you typically start your day? Roll out of bed, get dressed and scarf down some breakfast, right? Well, before you head out the door, spend some time with God. Reading the daily devotions in this book will just take a few minutes but will have an incredible influence!

You'll get a verse from God's Word that will help you focus your thoughts on Him, as well as a ChallengePoint – an action to work on. What a great way to start the day!

My prayer for you is that reading this book every day will grow your faith stronger and help you see how God cares about every area of your life!

God is fond of you.
If He had a wallet,
your photo would be in it.
If He had a refrigerator,
your picture would be on it.
He sends you flowers every
spring and a sunrise every
morning.Face it, friend,
He's crazy about you.

– Max Lucado

January

His Love

How precious are Your thoughts about me, O God. They cannot be numbered!

Psalm 139:17

God thinks about you so much that you can't even count how often. Does the idea that He is thinking about you make you feel like He's checking up on you? Well, that's not a very good way to feel, is it? No one wants to feel like someone is keeping an eye on them, especially if He's waiting for them to mess up or something.

This Scripture verse tells you that God thinks about you all the time. But He's not checking up on you. He thinks about you because He cares about what's going on in your life. Yeah ... He loves you.

ChallengePoint

God thinks about you ... so what? Don't feel nervous about that. Be thankful that He cares enough to think about you and wants to know what's going on in your life. You don't have to worry about problems or decisions you need to make. Just ask God for help and guidance – He's thinking about you anyway!

God is the one who began this good work in you, and I am certain that He won't stop before it is complete on the day that Christ Jesus returns.

Philippians 1:6

Are you a quitter? Do you start things and work like crazy for a while, but lose interest and quit before the job is finished? You know who doesn't quit? God! He started working in your heart the minute you met Him (even before that) to help you learn to be like Jesus.

He will never quit working on you because He loves you and wants what's best for you! Even if you disobey Him, even if you "quit" on Him, He will NEVER quit on you. He has a plan for you and He will keep right on working on it.

ChallengePoint

God must love you a lot, huh? He started working in your heart to help you become more like Jesus. He started working out a plan for what your future will be. No matter what kind of problems pop up, He will keep right on working. He's an expert in stick-to-it-ive-ness! The glue that makes that stick-to-it-ive-ness work is love!

Obeying Him

"Everyone who hears these words of Mine and puts them into practice is like a wise man who built his house on the rock."

Matthew 7:24

Two viewpoints:

1. Obeying is dumb and not cool in any way.
2. Obeying shows just how smart you really are.

The scoop here is that God knows best. Yep, that's it. God knows what is best for you and, since He loves you, He wants to let you in on that wisdom. Jesus makes it sound so simple ... if you learn to listen to His words and obey them when you're young, then you lay the groundwork or foundation for a whole lifetime of living for Him.

So – just like a house that is built on rock instead of sand – you'll be able to stand firm when things in life get hard, because you've learned to trust and obey God.

ChallengePoint

It takes a lot of character and strength to obey; especially when the guys around you do their own thing. Obeying isn't always easy but it IS always smart. Ask God to help you listen to His words, and learn.

Knowing God by
Showing Courage

God is our refuge and strength, an ever-present help in trouble.

Psalm 46:1

Refuge is kind of a funny word. You don't hear it much in normal conversation. Do you know what a refuge is? It is a hiding place ... a place where you are hidden and protected from danger. God is your safe hiding place. He protects you when danger comes and He gives you the strength and courage to get through the scary times. He wants to help you ... really ... God *wants* to help you.

This verse says God is an "ever-present help". That means He is standing at attention, keeping an eye on you and everything going on around you. He's like your guard and He will jump in to hide you, protect you and strengthen you. It's true – His Word says so!

ChallengePoint

OK, it's not cool to be afraid of things, but really, everyone is afraid of something. What scares you? God will be your refuge and strength; all you have to do is ask Him. Be honest with God. Tell Him what you are afraid of. Ask Him to hide you from it and strengthen you as you face it. He will. His Word promises that.

When I asked for Your help, You answered my prayer and gave me courage.

Psalm 138:3

When you cry out, it means you have a serious problem and need immediate help! God responds right away. He's always listening. He cares about what's going on in your life.

But does God always answer by doing what you want Him to do? Nope, you can't tell God what to do. So … if you can't tell Him what to do, how can you say that He answers prayer? 'Cause sometimes He responds like this:

⟶ You pray

⟶ Problems do not go away.

⟶ You have the strength to get through them.

⟶ God gave you that strength.

Cool.

ChallengePoint

Sometimes God doesn't take problems away, but He teaches you how to handle them by making you strong. Keep praying and pay attention to how God answers your prayers.

Knowing God by
Serving Him

"Do to others what you want them to do to you. This is the meaning of the law of Moses and the teaching of the prophets."

Matthew 7:12

You hit me and I'll hit back ... harder." Does that statement sound pretty fair to you? It is the way a lot of people choose to live, but it's not the way God teaches. He says to treat others the way you want them to treat you – and you go first.

So even if a friend or a brother is pounding you ... be nice. Is that easy? Nope, but it's the right thing to do. God says so. Anyone can be nice to people who are nice to them. But being nice first ... well, that's a different story. God cares about all people, so treating others with respect and love – no matter how they treat you – well, that's God's way.

ChallengePoint

No one said it would be easy. But God will help you be kind and loving, even to those who don't treat you that way. He's willing to help you do this, because it's the way He wants you to live. Need help? Just ask!

Giving

"Give, and you will receive. Your gift will return to you in full – pressed down, shaken together to make room for more, running over, and poured into your lap. The amount you give will determine the amount you get back."

Luke 6:38

There's an old saying that says, "You can't outgive God." So that means that if you give $5.00 in the offering at church, then you'll find $10.00 on the ground in the parking lot, right? WRONG. Here's the deal: Give all you can. Give money to God's work and to help the poor. Spend time helping others. Give energy to talk with people.

What do you get in return? The joy of knowing you've helped someone else and that you've obeyed God. You see, God doesn't really care about making you rich with things. He cares about making your heart more loving and kind, and helping you learn to live for Him.

ChallengePoint

Don't ever give just to see what you'll get back. You probably won't get anything because your heart is in the wrong place. That's sin, which cancels out the good you've done. Just give all you can and do it because you want to. Let God take care of what happens then.

Knowing God by
Abiding in Him

"You will search for Me. And when you search for Me with all your heart, you will find Me!"

Jeremiah 29:13

Do you like mysteries? Do you enjoy looking for clues and figuring out the solution? Well, this mystery is an easy one because it only has one clue. If you want to know God, really know Him, then you have to put your whole heart into it.

That sounds simple until you actually think about it. A lot of things are going to pull against you giving your whole heart to God. Friends will shout for attention and hobbies, sports and schoolwork all want some of your time. Satan is going to constantly throw things in front of you that tempt you to make them more important than God. If anything becomes more important than God, even for a little while, then your WHOLE heart isn't looking for Him.

ChallengePoint

No matter how strong you are, you can't do this on your own. Ask God to help you be strong in seeking Him. Ask Him to help you keep other things out of the way by noticing them and then pushing them back to where they should be – behind Him.

Enduring

I run with purpose in every step. I am not just shadowboxing. I discipline my body like an athlete, training it to do what it should. Otherwise, I fear that after preaching to others I myself might be disqualified.

1 Corinthians 9:26-27

Keep on keeping on" is the message here. When you decided to live for God, did you know that you would face opposition sometimes? Maybe you've figured that out by now. When you're trying to obey God and live for Him, you will face one problem after another because Satan wants to stop you. He doesn't want any success for God's team.

So what you do is fix your eyes on your goal and keep your focus there. Don't let anything pull your focus from the finish line, which is the goal of becoming more and more like Jesus.

ChallengePoint

Stick-to-it-ive-ness is the key here. Decide that you will obey God no matter what and don't let anything tempt you away from that. Then, run hard for the finish line, just like a competitor in a race, and don't let anything keep you from finishing strong. Live for God and obey Him – no matter what!

Being Like Christ

You must stop telling lies. Tell each other the truth, because we all belong to each other in the same body.

Ephesians 4:25

It starts like this:

- One little, teeny, tiny lie.
- One little, big, bigger lie to cover up that first one.
- One bigger lie to cover up the first two.
- Bigger. Bigger. Bigger.

Pretty soon it's hard to keep all your lies straight. Do people actually get up in the morning and think, "I'm going to tell a bazillion lies today." Probably not. So why do lies start in the first place? Usually for one of two reasons: To keep yourself out of trouble. Or to make you look good, important, or smart.

The problem is lying and loving don't go together, and God's instructions on how to live well is to love others as much as you love yourself.

ChallengePoint

Your model for living well is Jesus. He didn't lie. He always told the truth even when it was tough. It's not always easy to be honest but it's the right thing to do.

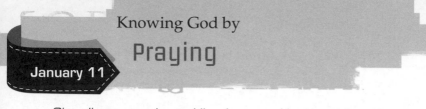

Give all your worries to Him, because He cares about you.
1 Peter 5:7

How cool is this: You can give your worries to God and He will take care of things so that you don't need to worry about anything. It's true. Memorize this Scripture verse so you always remember it.

You can tell God what's on your mind. Tell Him what worries you or scares you or what you can't get off your mind ... just tell Him. He cares about whatever is on your mind. Tell Him and let Him handle things. Just trust Him.

ChallengePoint

This sounds like it should be easy, but the truth is it's not. It's true that He cares about you and that He wants you to talk to Him. But when you tell God the things that are on your mind and ask Him to take care of them ... you have to let Him. You have to trust Him enough to let Him take care of them. That trust is something you have to learn through practice. So start practicing now!

Trusting Him

The LORD gives perfect peace to those whose faith is firm.
Isaiah 26:3

Peace? What does that even mean? Look around the world and you don't see much peace: You will see wars that have gone on for years; terrorists attacking at any moment; murders committed every day. Look at your own friends. How often is there some fight going on between them?

Now look at yourself. Do you have peace in your life? What is peace, you ask? It's contentment – a settledness with what's going on in your life. It's knowing that you don't have to worry about anything at all. That peace comes from knowing you can trust God completely.

ChallengePoint

True peace is not possible without trusting God. Do you believe that He loves you? Do you believe that He has a plan for your life and will guide you into that plan for your future? Do you know that He is watching over you and taking care of you? Peace means that you trust Him and that you don't have to worry about any wars and terrorists.

Using His Gifts

The sun has one kind of glory, while the moon and stars each have another kind. And even the stars differ from each other in their glory.

1 Corinthians 15:41

A good self-image means having confidence in your abilities and talents. It means knowing that God made you just the way you are. Even before you were born He knew what you would be like. God didn't use a cookie cutter and made everyone exactly the same.

Look at the sky; the sun has a job that is very important, but the moon and stars have jobs too. They are just as important as the sun. But they are different from the sun. God knew what He was doing when He made the world. And He knew what He was doing when He made you too.

ChallengePoint

There is a saying, "God don't make no junk." It's true. You may not know yet how you fit into God's plan, but if you keep searching you'll find out. God *did* make you unique. He did that because He has a plan for your life and how He wants to use you in His work. Look for the plan. Thank God for who you are!

Seeking His Protection

I will lie down and sleep in peace, for You alone, O LORD, make me dwell in safety.

Psalm 4:8

Y̶ou may not want to admit it but once in a while you get scared. Sometimes when you climb into bed and the room is dark, your mind starts running with all the nutty things you can possibly think about and you get scared. It's OK to be scared – in fact, it's smart to respect the evil forces in the world.

HOWEVER, you don't have to be so fearful that you can't sleep. God is more powerful than any force of evil and He will take care of you. He loves you. Even when you're sleeping, He is watching out for you. You can sleep in peace because you are safe.

ChallengePoint

Everyone wants to know they are safe. But there isn't any way to know that apart from God. Remember how powerful He is. Remember that He commands everything. Remember that nothing can stand against Him. Remember how much He loves you. He will take care of you. He is watching over you all the time. So close your eyes and sleep. You are safe.

"Come now, let's settle this," says the LORD. "Though your sins are like scarlet, I will make them as white as snow. Though they are red like crimson, I will make them as white as wool."

Isaiah 1:18

What's your reaction when someone cheats? What about when you get in an argument with someone? Do you want to get even? Do you want to win? Does forgiving the other person enter your mind at all?

Real forgiveness isn't easy. Oh sure, it's easy to say, "Yeah, I forgive you," but forgiveness that truly forgets about the wrong is not so easy. The memory of the wrong sticks in the back of your mind and then pops out again the next time you get mad. God does it though. When He forgives you, He washes away the sins. He makes you clean. That's complete forgiveness.

ChallengePoint

The privilege of being washed clean in God's sight can happen because Jesus died for your sins. When you accept Jesus as Savior, God sees you as clean. He is willing to forgive and forget your sins because of what Jesus did. That's amazing forgiveness. Model it by forgiving those who hurt or offend you.

Seeking His Guidance

"I know the plans I have for you," declares the LORD, "plans to prosper you and not to harm you, plans to give you hope and a future."

Jeremiah 29:11

What do you want to be when you grow up? Do you dream of playing in the NBA? How about being an archeologist or an astronaut? It's fun to dream about the future, isn't it? But when you think about it, do you wonder what your future will really hold?

There's a way to find out and to know for sure that it will be good – ask God to guide you. He wants to show you how to obey Him and serve Him. He will guide you into a wonderful life if you ask Him to. In fact, He wants you to ask!

ChallengePoint

God cares more about your heart obeying Him and loving Him than whether you are a professional athlete or a pilot or anything else. Of course, God will give you career guidance too, because He loves you. But God's guidance will lead you in learning ways to obey and serve Him, because He allows His children on earth to partner with Him in telling the world about His love.

Understanding Anger

In your anger do not sin: Do not let the sun go down while you are still angry.

Ephesians 4:26

Someone makes you mad ... really mad. You start thinking of ways to get even or maybe you even give him a punch. When you're REALLY mad, you might lie in bed at night thinking about how mad you are. You probably won't get much sleep then.

This is NOT the way God wants you to handle your anger. He doesn't tell you not to get angry. He says to be careful how you handle your anger – don't sin and settle it right away. Talk with whoever made you angry and sort it out.

God knows that if you let the anger roll around inside you it is only going to cause more problems and mess up friendships and relationships. Those matter to Him – He says it's important to love one another.

ChallengePoint

Control your anger. If you can't do this, ask God to help you. God's Word instructs you to love others and that's hard to do when you're super-mad at them. So settle situations quickly and get on with the good things in life.

His Faithfulness

January 18

Great is His faithfulness; His mercies begin afresh each morning.

Lamentations 3:23

God never gets tired of loving you. He never gives up on you. It doesn't matter how often you do things that are hurtful to Him or to someone else. He just keeps on loving you.

Stop and think about it and you will realize that every morning God blesses you with a new day, love of family, food to eat, friends to hang out with, new experiences ... a multitude of blessings. Every day! God doesn't get disgusted with your disobedience and walk away, He is faithful to care for you and love you every day.

ChallengePoint

What should your response be to God's faithfulness? Confessing your sins to Him and telling Him you're sorry for them. Ask for His help to live more obediently to Him each day. God's faithfulness to you is daily, so make every attempt to make your faithfulness to Him a daily effort too.

Knowing God by

Seeking Salvation

Jesus answered, "I am the way, and the truth, and the life. No one comes to the Father except through Me."

John 14:6

A map shows you how to get from Point A to Point B. Follow the roads shown on the map and you will get to where you want to go. The Bible has a map in it too. Its map shows you how to find a personal relationship with Jesus and be able to know that you can go to heaven someday.

Everyone needs to be saved to go to heaven. That's because all people are sinners and no sin is allowed in heaven. That means people have to be cleaned up. Salvation is possible because Jesus died on the cross for all sins. When you accept Jesus as your Savior, your sins are washed away and you can go to heaven.

ChallengePoint

There is only one way to salvation – through Jesus. Ask Him to be your Savior and to forgive your sins. When you've done that, you can KNOW that you are saved and will one day be in heaven with Him.

Being Thankful

*Sing praises to the L*ORD*; praise our God with harps.*

Psalm 147:7

Here's an idea: When someone does something nice for you ... say thank you. And mean it. It feels good to be thanked, doesn't it? Think about it, when you do something nice, you're a lot more willing to do it again if the person remembers to thank you.

Guess what? God likes to be thanked too. He does so much for you every day. In fact, He does so much that people take a lot of His gifts for granted. They seem to think they deserve them. The truth is that no one deserves anything God does – His gifts come from His kind and loving heart.

ChallengePoint

Stop right now and make a list of the gifts God gives you each day. Don't forget things like sunshine, oxygen, rain and family. When you see how long your list is, you will want to stop and thank God for all He gives you. Your list will let you see how much He loves you. What an amazing God!

Celebrating Him

Let everything that breathes praise the LORD. Praise the LORD!

Psalm 150:6

When you hear something over and over it can stop being special news. If you grew up in a Christian home, with parents who pray with you and read the Bible to you, then you have heard about God's amazing love.

If you've started thinking about His love in a ho-hum kind of way then you need to wake up the way you're thinking! Think about how much energy people put into celebrating a victory by their favorite sports team or winning in a favorite video game. Celebrating who God is and what He does for you should be a zillion times greater!

ChallengePoint

The only way you're going to get pumped enough to celebrate God is by getting to know Him and under-standing all He has done for you and all He does EVERY DAY! Read His Word ... really read it so that you understand it. Get to know Him by really thinking about His love. When you do that – you will celebrate like never before!

"I say to you, love your enemies. Pray for those who hurt you. If you do this, you will be true children of your Father in heaven. He causes the sun to rise on good people and on evil people, and He sends rain to those who do right and to those who do wrong."

Matthew 5:44-45

OK, be honest ... how do you treat your enemies? Do you want the best for them? Do you PRAY for them? Yeah, probably not. But if you are learning to live and act like God, then you are learning to love all people – even the ones who are mean to you.

Is it easy? No, it isn't. But the good thing is that you don't have to do it alone. God wants you to learn to be loving and He knows it's hard. So He will help you. Just ask Him.

ChallengePoint

Loving other people – even your enemies – is what makes you more like God. Read God's Word and find the promises of how He will help you learn to be forgiving and loving. He will help you find the good in people, even when they aren't nice to you.

Suppressing My Pride

You save the humble, but You bring down those who are proud.

Psalm 18:27

"Yay me! Let me tell you how smart I am and what a great athlete I am. Everyone likes me ... I'm AWESOME!" That, my friend, is bragging. No one likes to hear someone constantly talking about how great he is. When a guy brags, it puts other people down and lifts the bragger above everyone else.

God is not a fan of bragging. He's supportive of humble people. The difference between the humble and the proud (braggers) is that humble people celebrate the victories and successes of other people. God wants your focus to be on others – loving others more than you love yourself. Bragging about yourself doesn't fit with that. Loving others means being happy for their successes.

ChallengePoint

One of the characteristics of obeying God is humility, which lifts other people up when they do better than you do or even win over you. There is no room for bragging when you are following God. Love and pride can't live in the same place. What are you going to do about that?

Come close to God, and God will come close to you. Wash your hands, you sinners; purify your hearts, for your loyalty is divided between God and the world.

James 4:8

OK, here's a test ... pick up a piece of paper. Look at the front of the paper. Look at the back of the paper. Now, separate the back from the front ... go ahead, just pull it apart. Can't do it, huh?

Now you know what abiding is like – sticking so close to God that you're like two sides of the same piece of paper. It's hanging on tight, with both hands! Why? 'Cause God loves you that much. He wants to be that close to you so that you get to know Him as well as you can. That only happens by abiding.

ChallengePoint

One thing about abiding with God though ... you have to be cleaned up before you can be that close to Him. Confess your sins, and clean up your act so that you can be in His presence. God is clean and pure and can't be in the presence of dirt. Stick close to Him and you will begin to feel the same way.

> *"Come to Me, all of you who are tired and have heavy loads, and I will give you rest."*
>
> *Matthew 11:28*

What's the biggest problem you face? Maybe it's dealing with a tough home situation because your parents are divorced, or they're together but fight all the time. Maybe your family has financial trouble and that pressure lays on you like a heavy blanket.

These kinds of pressures can make you feel like you're carrying a 100-pound load on your back. How do you get out from under those heavy burdens? Go to Jesus. He said it, "Come to Me ..."

ChallengePoint

There is nothing – absolutely nothing you face in life that Jesus doesn't know about. He knows if you're overwhelmed with all that you have to face. He not only knows, He cares, and He offers to lift your load. How does He do that? Different ways – sometimes He changes your attitude. Sometimes He reminds you that He's in control and can handle things. Other times He brings people around you to encourage you. The bottom line is that He cares and He will help you if you come to Him.

Using His Gifts

January 26

Don't be concerned about the outward beauty of fancy hairstyles, expensive jewelry, or beautiful clothes. You should clothe yourselves instead with the beauty that comes from within, the unfading beauty of a gentle and quiet spirit, which is so precious to God.

1 Peter 3:3-4

Does this verse sound "girly" to you? After all, you're not into fancy hairstyles or expensive jewelry, are you? OK, substitute in expensive basketball shoes or the brand of jeans that all the guys wear or the coolest skateboard known to man. Now, does that fit you better?

The point of this verse is ... don't spend so much time on outward stuff that you forget the inward stuff.

ChallengePoint

God cares a whole lot more about how you treat other people than whether or not you're stylin' with the latest, most expensive stuff. How you treat others shows what kind of stuff is living in your heart. What He wants to see is your desire to obey Him and learn to be more and more like Jesus. That's what makes you look good to God.

Knowing God by

His Love

January 27

The LORD is compassionate and gracious, slow to anger, abounding in love.

Psalm 103:8

Maybe you've heard that God loves you so often that it doesn't really mean anything anymore. Stop and think about this description of how God shows His love ... this may really wake you up to His love.

- God is compassionate. That means that He feels sympathy for you when you're suffering. He cares. Not only does He care ... He wants to help you.
- God is gracious. That means that He is kind and generous. He gives and forgives because of His graciousness.
- God is slow to anger. Wow. Think about that. He loves you so He gives you the benefit of the doubt and He gives you chance after chance to obey Him.
- God is abounding in love. That means that He loves and loves and loves ... more than you can imagine.

ChallengePoint

God is love. He says that about Himself. It's impossible to understand how much He loves you. He cares about you, gives to you, and doesn't get angry with you.

Praying to Him

Whenever they were in trouble and turned to the LORD, the God of Israel, and sought Him out, they found Him.

2 Chronicles 15:4

Trouble happens and it happens all too often. What do you do when you're in trouble? There are a few options: try to hide whatever wrong you've done. Blame it on someone else. Cry ... sorry, you DON'T cry, right?

But what's the best option when you're in trouble? It makes the most sense to get help. Getting help from someone you trust is the smartest thing. The best Person to turn to is God. When you're in trouble and you look for Him by reading His Word, talking to Him, listening to Him – you'll find Him.

ChallengePoint

There are two important things about today's Scripture verse: one is that you need to seek God. Don't yell for help if you aren't doing your part of reading the Bible and praying. And, secondly, when you look for Him, you WILL find Him. Cool, huh?

Knowing God by

Seeking His Protection

You are my hiding place; You will protect me from trouble; and surround me with songs of deliverance.

Psalm 32:7

Long ago knights fought hand-to-hand battles wearing heavy armor. Even famous King Saul in the Bible had armor that he offered to David before the young boy left to fight the giant, Goliath. Armor protects the body from being injured. It keeps the wearer safe.

God is like armor for your soul. How does He do it? He surrounds you, protecting you from trouble. He deflects attacks by Satan on you. There is nothing and no one who is stronger or more powerful than God.

ChallengePoint

So how do you get this God-armor that will keep you safe? Just as God protected the psalmist, He will protect you too. In order to put this armor on, all you have to do is ask for it. Ask God for His protection and then make yourself available to Him. He will give you protection. He's waiting for you.

"No one can serve two masters. For you will hate one and love the other; you will be devoted to one and despise the other. You cannot serve both God and money."

Luke 16:13

Magnets are pretty fun to play with. When you hold the opposite poles of two magnets toward each other they slam together tightly. But when you hold the wrong sides toward each other, they fight coming together. You have to force them to get them to touch and they definitely will not stay together.

That fight of two magnets pushing away from each other is what happens when you try to live as though God AND something else is most important to you. Besides, you will quickly find out that it's impossible to give all your energy and attention to two different things – especially when they are opposites.

ChallengePoint

God wants to be the most important thing in your world and He doesn't share that #1 spot with anyone else. It's OK if you have friends and hobbies and a job someday … but NOTHING should be more important to you than God. Nothing.

We may think we are doing the right thing, but the LORD always knows what is in our hearts.

Proverbs 21:2

Are you a champion excuse giver? Can you usually point to things someone else does that actually cause you to do what you do? Yeah, then things are never your fault, right? Your motives are always good and pure. Right.

See, you may be able to fake that with other people. You can justify your actions every day, but you can never fool God. Sorry, but He knows what's going on in your heart. He knows your real motives.

ChallengePoint

Why does God look at your motives? Because He cares about what's going on in your heart. If you're constantly making excuses for your bad behavior or your attitudes, that means your heart is not loving and obeying God. If God has control of your heart so that you want to live for Him and please Him, you won't need to make excuses for anything.

God loves each one of us
as if there were only one of us.
– St. Augustine

February

Confessing Sin

Finally, I confessed all my sins to You and stopped trying to hide my guilt. I said to myself, "I will confess my rebellion to the LORD." And You forgave me! All my guilt is gone.

Psalm 32:5

This is the coolest thing ever – God does NOT want you to feel guilty all the time! He knows you do wrong things ... you know it too. He knows that it is hard to obey all the time ... you have a sinful nature and it comes out sometimes. He knows you're sometimes going to feel guilty for the way you act and the things you think, so, He made a way to get the guilt off your back – confession.

What does that mean? It means coming clean – telling God when you sin. Just admit it and don't try to hide it. Let's face it; you don't really think you can hide things from God anyway, do you? Confess it and He will forgive you. He promised. Cool, huh?

ChallengePoint

Let's be honest – confession isn't easy. Some of us think that we can hide our sins from God (and everyone else). Confessing them just makes them real. However, confessing will lift guilt off of you. Guilt is not a fun thing to carry around. Why not just confess and accept God's forgiveness? Then guilt has no power over you!

Finally, my friends, keep your minds on whatever is true, pure, right, holy, friendly, and proper. Don't ever stop thinking about what is truly worthwhile and worthy of praise.

Philippians 4:8

Okay, you're just a kid, so you probably don't think much about needing guidance for your life yet. That may seem like something that is more for grown-ups. But did you know that God wants to give you guidance in your life right now? Yep, He wants to guide you in how to live for Him and obey Him. He wants to guide you in how to treat other people and in doing His work in your world.

However, He can't really do that guiding if you aren't doing your part. Your part is to put your mind in a place that honors Him. He won't guide you if your thoughts are all about how to cheat, hurt, disrespect and dishonor others. What would be the point?

ChallengePoint

Do you want God's guidance in your life ... starting now? Then keep your thoughts on things that show you're serious about obeying Him. Think about things that honor Him and then see His guidance show up in your life through your thoughts.

Understanding Anger

My dear brothers and sisters, always be willing to listen and slow to speak. Do not become angry easily, because anger will not help you live the right kind of life God wants.

James 1:19-20

What do you do when you get angry? Stomp off in a huff? Throw things? Yell? Anger doesn't usually show itself in calm, quiet ways. But everyone gets angry sometimes; it's to be expected, right? Well then, why does God care so much about human anger? He cares because He has given a lot of instruction about how people should treat each other – and none of them include getting angry.

God wants people to really listen to each other. Listen quietly, with respect. Control your anger so it doesn't explode in someone else's face. Treat people with love, kindness and respect.

ChallengePoint

Granted, it's a lot easier to control your anger with some people than it is with others. But those people you are most likely to get angry with are the ones you most need to control yourself around ... bummer, huh? So, how are you going to do it? Read the verse again – listen, keep your mouth shut, and don't jump to reactions that make you angry. OK, maybe you should ask God for help.

Knowing God by

His Faithfulness

Know therefore that the LORD your God is God; He is the faithful God, keeping His covenant of love to a thousand generations of those who love Him and keep His commands.

Deuteronomy 7:9

Cross my heart" used to be the words that sealed a promise. If someone made a promise to you and sealed it with those words, you knew you could bank on them keeping that promise. Of course ... sometimes they didn't.

Most people are pretty trustworthy and make every effort to keep their promises but sometimes, because of situations that develop or a promise made foolishly, well, it just isn't possible. Except for one Person – God. Yep, He is faithful and that means absolutely NOTHING will stop Him from keeping every promise He has made. Get it? NOTHING. Read His Word to learn what those promises are – one of them is to love you totally!

ChallengePoint

So what does it mean to you that God is faithful? He has promised to love you, guide you, protect you, use you in His work, and a multitude of other promises. Read His Word to discover them. Then start trusting Him. If He said it you can bank on it.

Seeking Salvation

"For God so loved the world that He gave His one and only Son, that whoever believes in Him shall not perish but have eternal life."

John 3:16

A coach prepares his team for a big game by coming up with a game plan. That plan will be their strategy to hopefully win the game. Did you know God has a game plan too? His game plan makes it possible for you to come to heaven someday and live forever with Him.

God's game plan is way more important than just winning a game. It cost Him something – Jesus, His only Son. God's goal was to make eternal life possible for all people, because He loves all people. The only way that could happen was if the sins of all people were paid for somehow. Jesus' death on the cross paid for our sins and that makes eternal life with God possible. Good game plan, wouldn't you say?

ChallengePoint

The only way God's game plan means anything is if you accept it. When you confess your sins and ask Jesus into your heart, then you are saved. God's game plan has then worked for you. It's up to you to take action.

Being Thankful

Always use the name of our Lord Jesus Christ to thank God the Father for everything.

Ephesians 5:20

Everyone likes to be thanked once in a while. If you make it a point to do something nice for someone, it makes you feel appreciated when they take the time to say thanks. But God is bigger than people and He has a better self-image than people, right? So why does He need to be thanked for stuff?

You know, it isn't so much that He needs to be thanked, it's more that when you take time to thank Him for everything He does for you and everything He gives you, then you start thinking about that stuff and you realize how much He cares for you. Actually saying thanks, even before you feel it, gives you time to think about Him ... then you will really FEEL thankful too.

ChallengePoint

Take some time and make a list of everything God does for you. Tell Him you're thankful, even if you don't really feel that in your heart yet. Let the thankfulness grow as you understand how much and how often He shows His love to you.

Celebrating Him

You are worthy, O Lord our God, to receive glory and honor and power. For You created all things, and they exist because You created what You pleased.

Revelation 4:11

Celebrate God! Maybe you wonder what that even means. Well, break it down. When do you celebrate? When something good has happened, such as winning a big game or coming in first in a big contest. You also celebrate happy occasions like birthdays.

Celebrations usually involve a big party, lots of food and definitely fun. It's a time of appreciation, right? Well, why not do that for God? He created everything there is on this earth and He made it all from nothing! If that doesn't deserve a celebration, what does?

ChallengePoint

Throw a party! Blow noisemakers! Toss confetti! Celebrate who God is and His incredible imagination and creativity. Celebrate His love! Celebrate His guidance! Celebrate the salvation He makes possible! Celebrate Him! As you celebrate all He is and all He does, you will come to understand and appreciate Him more.

Enduring

"Lead us not into temptation, but deliver us from the evil one."

Matthew 6:13

Life is going along great. Then all of a sudden, some big, old temptation pops its head up in front of you and things begin to fall apart. What's a temptation? Something like, "Hey kid, cheat on this test. No one will know." Or, "Make fun of that new guy. He's a geek anyway." Or, "Obey your parents? Get real. Just tell them to take a hike!"

What do you do when you're tempted to do something that deep down inside you know is wrong? Pray this prayer (part of the Lord's Prayer) and ask God to help you be strong. Guess what? It's His nature to always help you and to always be there for you. You can endure temptation (that means you can face it but not give in to it) because of His strength in you.

ChallengePoint

Ask Him for strength to stand against temptations. Ask God for help to be kind, loving and obedient. Then recognize when He helps you in the way you have asked. When you see how He comes through for you, then you'll trust Him more the next time.

> "If you want good fruit, you must make the tree good. If
> your tree is not good, it will have bad fruit. A tree is known
> by the kind of fruit it produces."
>
> Matthew 12:33

Members of a team usually have something that identifies them as belonging together – like matching shirts or uniforms. What identifies you as belonging to God's team? The more you act, think, and make choices like Christ, the more you show that you are on God's team.

Yeah, you can say all the right "Christian" words and even quote Bible verses, but if the way you treat others doesn't match your words, well, that's the bad fruit this verse is talking about.

How do you learn to be like Christ? Get to know Him – read about His life in the Gospels. See how He honored God, how He treated people, and how He spent His time. As you learn about Him you'll learn how you should live your life.

ChallengePoint

It's a high goal to be like Christ all the time. In fact, it is impossible, but still something to strive for. Remember that what's in your heart (good or evil) will come out in the way you live. Learn to know God well.

Loving Others

"Your love for one another will prove to the world that you are My disciples."

John 13:35

Love, love, love. Why does the Bible talk so much about love and mushy stuff like that? OK, admittedly love is not something guys talk about a lot. But it is an important topic in the Bible. Why? Simple – God wants people to love each other, because He loves all people.

When you love others – even those who are a pain in the neck and are just downright hard to love – then you are showing a family likeness to God. Anyone can love their friends, but when you love all people it shows that God is in your life. You are showing His love to others by loving them yourself.

ChallengePoint

There's no doubt that some people are hard to love. In fact, if you had to love them with your own strength you know it would never happen. But with God in your heart, loving those people becomes possible. God is love, let Him love through you!

Showing Courage

The LORD is my light and my salvation – whom shall I fear?
The LORD is the stronghold of my life – of whom shall I be
afraid?

Psalm 27:1

Most guys don't like to admit that they are scared of anything. Maybe you're like that. But deep in your heart, you have to admit that there are a couple of things that really frighten you. That's OK, you don't have to tell anyone except yourself and God.

Everyone is scared of something. What does knowing God have to do with fear? Knowing God makes you realize that with God in your life there is really nothing to be afraid of, because He can and will protect you from whatever dangers come into your life. God is more powerful than anything else in the world. So what is there to be afraid of?

ChallengePoint

Stop for a minute and think about God's power that created everything there is. Think about the power of nature which God controls, the power of ocean waves, lightning and wind. Think about His power that raised Christ from the dead. All of that power is available to you, you must just ask.

Giving

Each of you has received a gift to use to serve others. Be good servants of God's various gifts of grace.

1 Peter 4:10

Who do you most admire? Some famous athlete? An artist? A musician? Whoever it is, just imagine that your hero walked up to you one day and said, "Hey, Dude, will you help me play this next game (or paint this portrait or write this song)?" Yeah, right … like little old you could do anything to help this star accomplish something in his own special field.

God thinks you can – no, He KNOWS you can. God has this gigantic supply of abilities and gifts that He passes out to each person here on earth. The reason? It's incredible, but God wants our help to get His work done here on earth. Yep, He lets us plain human beings help Him with His plans for the earth.

ChallengePoint

Do you find it amazing that God believes you have something to offer His work? Well, He does and He has given you the abilities and talents to do what He would like. Are you willing to give God your time and energy?

Knowing God by

Trusting Him

The LORD is my strength and my shield; my heart trusts in Him, and I am helped. My heart leaps for joy and I will give thanks to Him in song.

Psalm 28:7

Do you often burst out in song? How often do you burst out in song when you're afraid or troubled? It's harder to sing then, isn't it?

The thing about trust is that trust is only trust in the hard times of life. Get it? Anyone can claim to trust God and sing about it when things are going great. But if life is really stinky and you believe that God will get you through – that's trust. If you believe in God's strength, power, love and protection, then you are trusting Him.

ChallengePoint

OK, honesty time. Think about a hard time in your life: Family problems, illness, death of a loved one, moving to a new school … whatever it might be. What was your first reaction in that situation? Panic? Fear? Assurance that God knows about it and will get you through it? The last one is the one to work toward. If you don't go right to that place every time, that's OK. You will get there eventually, and the more you experience trust the more you will be able to trust.

His Love

I am convinced that nothing can ever separate us from God's love. Neither death nor life, neither angels nor demons, neither our fears for today nor our worries about tomorrow – not even the powers of hell can separate us from God's love.

Romans 8:38

Have you ever had a friend get mad at you and just decide he doesn't want to be your friend anymore? Stinks, huh? Along the same lines, how does it feel when someone you love dies? Stinks even more. When love stops being love, it hurts, especially if someone chooses to take their love away.

Guess what? God will NEVER do that. He never stops loving you. More importantly, NOTHING and NO ONE can ever pull you away from His love. His love for you is so strong, steady and constant that no power on earth, no demon, angel, storm ... NOTHING can separate you from Him.

ChallengePoint

Yes, it's true that nothing can separate you from God's love. The ONLY thing that can get in the way of God's love for you is ... you. Yep, His love is there for you to receive and enjoy. So ... do you receive it?

Praying

"Ask and it will be given to you; seek and you will find; knock and the door will be opened to you."

Matthew 7:7

Does this verse mean that you can nag God into giving you what you want? Seriously, can you bug Him until He gives you the latest video game or the coolest pair of basketball shoes? Yeah, not likely. So what does this verse mean? Asking God for help shows your dependence on Him, and God wants you to depend on Him. He wants you to keep asking Him for the desires of your heart.

But when you constantly talk to God and read His Word your desires start to change. As you get to know Him better and spend more time with Him, your heart tends to become more like His. This Scripture verse is written to people who know God; those who want to grow hearts like His.

ChallengePoint

The first step is to know God. Once you know God, tell Him the desires of your heart – and keep on telling Him. Read His Word, think about Him and notice how He grows your heart to be like His. Knowing God by prayer makes you more like Him.

Seeking His Protection

February 16

We know that in everything God works for the good of those who love Him. They are the people He called, because that was His plan.

Romans 8:28

You lose a big game, fail a test, fight with a friend, get grounded ... sometimes life is hard. Where is God when life stinks? He's where He's always been – with you.

God doesn't cause bad things to happen, but He will teach and guide you through them. He can redeem those tough situations. That means He will turn them into something good. Why would God do that? Because He loves you and wants to teach you to be a better person and a stronger Christian. He has work for you to do that will spread His message of love to those around you.

No experience – good or bad – is wasted. God will teach you through all of it. Yeah, sometimes the good He brings from a tough thing is just that you learn something about living for Him, loving Him and loving others.

ChallengePoint

When life gets tough, what should you do? Get depressed or angry? Instead, try looking for God's guidance. Be patient and see what good He will make from the situation.

Knowing God by

Serving Him

February 17

Feed the hungry and help those in trouble. Then your light will shine out from the darkness, and the darkness around you will be as bright as noon.

Isaiah 58:10

Every so often some natural disaster nearly wipes out some part of the world. Tsunamis in Indonesia, earthquakes in China, and hurricanes in the U.S. are just a few examples. When those things happen, Christians around the world gather to pray for those who lost their homes, family members and virtually everything they own.

Praying is good and certainly an important part of caring for others. But God expects more from His people. When someone is hungry or homeless or ill or has some other problem, and you have the ability to help them ... you'd better help.

ChallengePoint

The Bible says the second most important commandment is to love others. That means helping them when you can. Now, of course, as a kid there are some things you can't do. But as God's child you can work with others and even motivate others to help people in need in practical ways. Some people call this, "putting feet on your faith."

Obeying Him

"Don't worship any other god, because I, the LORD, the Jealous One, am a jealous God."

Exodus 34:14

What does obeying have to do with God being jealous? It's nearly impossible to obey God all the time, so what's the big deal, right? The big deal is who your heart belongs to. As this Scripture verse says, God insists on being #1 in your heart – the most important, the One you honor, respect, follow and obey.

If your heart isn't worshiping God and doesn't belong completely to Him then you will say, "Yeah, I love God," but then you'll think about things that don't honor Him. You'll be selfish or mean to others. In other words, you will not really serve and love Him. God won't stand for that. He wants all your heart and all your worship.

ChallengePoint

Honesty time – do you love God more than anything? Do you want to serve Him more than anything? Is He #1 in your life? If He's not, you're wasting your time. He is a jealous God and will only accept the #1 position.

Confessing Sin

If we confess our sins, He will forgive our sins, because we can trust God to do what is right. He will cleanse us from all the wrongs we have done.

1 John 1:9

You're tossing a ball in the house and your mom's favorite lamp gets knocked over and shatters on the floor. You did it. You know the rule is no balls in the house. But when Mom comes rushing in, what do you do? Blame the dog? Blame your little brother? Say, "It was an earthquake, Mom. It shook the lamp right off the table."

You might try the same kind of excuse making with God when you've done something wrong. But you won't fool Him. Making excuses means you have to carry around guilt and keep hiding the truth. The thing is, God wants to forgive you for your sins – even for lying to your Mom – but before He can do that, you have to admit them to Him.

ChallengePoint

Confession gets things out in the open. It clears the air so you can come to God and He can forgive you. Your relationship with Him, which was blocked because of your sin, is wide open again. God loves you. He wants to forgive your sins and wipe the slate clean.

His Forgiveness

Be kind and loving to each other, and forgive each other just as God forgave you in Christ.

Ephesians 4:32

O God, I messed up big time. Please forgive me. Please, please." Have you ever said a prayer like that? Sure, we all have. We pray those kinds of prayers with confidence that God will forgive us. He promised He would, because He loves us.

Yeah, but what happens when someone does you wrong? If he admits he did wrong and asks you to forgive him, do you? OK, honestly – maybe you do sometimes and maybe you don't sometimes.

What is there to learn about knowing God from this? God is loving, kind and forgiving to you. He says you are made in His image and that His desire is for you to treat other people with love and kindness. So it only makes sense that God would like you to pass along the love and kindness you experience from Him to others.

ChallengePoint

How good are you at forgiving others? It takes an un-selfish viewpoint to accept someone's apology and then honestly forgive them. Make it your goal to focus on loving others the way God loves you.

Seeking His Guidance

Trust in the LORD with all your heart; do not depend on your own understanding. Seek His will in all you do, and He will show you which path to take.

Proverbs 3:5-6

The cool thing about God is that He never leaves you on your own. He loves you so He keeps an eye on you all the time. Nothing that happens in your life – good or bad – surprises Him. That could seem a little freaky if you aren't living for Him. But it's really a good thing because it means you don't have to figure things out for yourself.

When you ask Him for guidance, He will show you what to do. That's a whole lot better than trying to figure things out for yourself, because God sees a much bigger picture than you do. You might be trying to solve a problem today, but He knows what you're going to need tomorrow, next week and next year. God loves you enough to see the big picture and guide you through it.

ChallengePoint

Do you love Him enough to trust Him? Yeah, that's the hard part – asking God for help, and then waiting for Him to show you what to do. Be patient, wait for Him to tell you what to do. He's a lot smarter than you are!

A fool shows his annoyance at once, but a prudent man overlooks an insult.

Proverbs 12:16

Imagine a quiet pool full of water. The water is so still that it's almost like a mirror reflecting your face as you look into it. But suddenly someone smashes a hand down on the water. Immediately it splashes in your face. The quiet reflection is gone as the water rolls and bubbles.

That's kind of what a quick temper is like. It explodes when you're not expecting it. A person with a quick temper does not stay calm; especially when something insulting is said to them. Maybe you think it's OK to explode if someone insults you. Sorry, but God says that's not the way it should be. A fool explodes – a wise dude stays calm. Why? 'Cause that shows your value comes from God, not from people, and because it shows that you want to please and honor God. That's wise.

ChallengePoint

Honesty time – are you an exploder or a calm dude? If you have a tendency to explode then maybe you need to work on finding your value from God and ask Him to help you be calmer and less reactive to situations. Be wise – stay calm.

His Faithfulness

"I have told you this, so that you might have peace in your hearts because of Me. While you are in the world, you will have to suffer. But cheer up! I have defeated the world."

John 16:33

What does the word *faithfulness* mean to you? It's probably not a word you use a lot. In relation to this Scripture verse, think of faithfulness like a safety net that is always under you, no matter what troubles you have. Life can get pretty tough sometimes – but God is faithful.

That means He is right there with you through all of your problems and sorrows. He may not stop them from happening, but He will walk through them with you and give you the strength and courage to face them. He's more powerful than any problem you may have. Trust Him to see you through.

ChallengePoint

It's easy to say, "Just trust God." But let's be honest, it isn't easy to trust that something good will come out of a really painful problem. Having a history with God where you can look back and see how He has been faithful in the past helps you trust Him more with current problems. So if you're facing a big problem right now, look back and see how God helped you in the past.

Seeking Salvation

The payment for sin is death. But God gives us the free gift of life forever in Christ Jesus our Lord.

Romans 6:23

Everyone sins. That's the bottom line. You can deny it or try to justify your actions, but the plain old truth is that you sin – you do things that break God's laws. Sin is serious and, just like when you disobey your parents and get punished, there is punishment for sin – death. Whoa! That IS serious.

Yep, God doesn't fool around when it comes to sin. You sin; you die forever – no heaven. WAIT A MINUTE! God loves people. God loves you. He offers the gift of life forever with Him. The gift is free to you. It cost Him something – the suffering and life of His only Son – but He did it anyway. Why? Because ... HE LOVES YOU!

ChallengePoint

Salvation is possible only because God loves you. It's available only because Jesus was willing to pay the price for your sins. It's free because that's how much God loves you. He wants you to be with Him forever in heaven ... alive. That's salvation and it saves you from the death caused by your sins.

Being Thankful

It is good to give thanks to the LORD, to sing praises to the Most High. It is good to proclaim Your unfailing love in the morning, Your faithfulness in the evening.

Psalm 92:1-2

Why does God want your thanks? After all ... He's the Creator of everything so He knows how awesome He is. Think about it ... if the first thing you think about every morning is thanking God for His love, and the last thing you think about before slipping into dreamland is His faithfulness, then chances are you will think about Him a few times during the day. You'll think about loving Him and living for Him.

Thankfulness also means you will appreciate all God does for you and how much He gives you. God knows that by reminding you to be thankful, you will be encouraged to grow in your love and faithfulness to Him.

ChallengePoint

Saying thanks is such a simple thing, really. So why not commit to start your day with thanking God for His love? Thank Him for some specific way He shows His love to you. End your day with thanks to Him too. See how your relationship with Him grows and changes as you live in thankfulness.

Celebrating Him

Clap your hands, all you people. Shout to God with joy.

Psalm 47:1

Do you need some ideas as to what you should celebrate about God? Here's a list to get you started:

He created everything ... EVERYTHING. That means:

- The earth, the sun, the moon, the stars.
- The oceans, the mountains, trees, flowers, grass.
- Every animal you can think of.
- Air and water.
- People – that means YOU – your family, and your friends.
- He sent Jesus, which means you can have salvation.
- The Bible and prayer.

Well, that should get you started. Celebrate God and all He gives!

ChallengePoint

Don't take any of God's many, many gifts for granted. Celebrate all the ways He shows His love to you!

> *We can rejoice, too, when we run into problems and trials, for we know that they help us develop endurance. And endurance develops strength of character, and character strengthens our confident hope of salvation.*
>
> Romans 5:3-5

Have your parents ever punished you and, as they were laying out the punishment, said, "This hurts us more than it does you"? Did you think, "Yeah, right"? As strange as it may seem to you, they were probably telling you the truth. Sometimes when you disobey they have to punish you because that's how you'll learn from your mistake. It makes them sad, but it's the right thing to do.

Does it surprise you to know that is also true in your relationship with God? He loves you so He wants you to grow into a mature, wise young man. However, the only way that maturity is going to come is through what you learn from problems and tough times. So when things get hard, learn all you can from your problems.

ChallengePoint

OK, admittedly it is not easy to be happy about problems. No one likes to suffer. So we won't ask you to celebrate trials. Just try to understand how God is growing you into a stronger and more responsible guy.

Knowing God by
Being Like Christ

Set your minds on things above, not on earthly things.

Colossians 3:2

So ... you're supposed to think about Jesus, angels, harps and clouds instead of baseball, your friends, or favorite snacks? Is that what this verse means? Not exactly. You see, the thing is that whatever fills your thoughts most of the time is going to show in how you live and in what you consider to be important. So, if beating up your little brother and squashing any happiness he has is often on your mind, you will probably end up doing that.

What did Christ think about when He was on earth? How to help others know God better. How to show kindness and love to them. He pretty much focused all of His thoughts on those areas. He did not think about Himself. If being like Christ and showing love to others, being helpful and kind is on your mind, well, that's the kind of stuff you'll do. So, think on the things of heaven – the things that will make you more like Christ.

ChallengePoint

Does this sound hard? Well, things that are worthwhile usually take some effort. A good starting place is to fill your thoughts with things that honor God and not just things that please you.

A smile is a curve that sets
everything straight.
– Anonymous

March

Loving Others

March 1

*No one has ever seen God. But if we love each other, God
lives in us, and His love is brought to full expression in us.*

1 John 4:12

Look around at your classmates, neighbors and friends.
Do any of them look like God? OK, do YOU look like
God? Maybe you think it's kind of hard to answer that
since no one has ever seen God, so how would you know
if someone looked like Him?

Actually, there's an easy way to answer that. Think
about people you enjoy spending time with. More than
likely they are people who are unselfish and kind –
people who show love to others. So ... guess what? They
look like God. You see, God loves people. Of course, He
wants people to obey Him and love Him back, but He
keeps on loving them even if they don't. So people show
what God is like by loving others.

ChallengePoint

Do you love other people? We're not talking mushy,
lovey-dovey kind of love. We're talking about "being nice,
unselfish and considerate" kind of love. You can do that.
Of course, it's easy with your friends, but what about
loving people who don't treat you nicely? Yeah, that's
when it gets hard. But that's when it counts most.

Showing Courage

Because He Himself suffered when He was tempted, He is able to help those who are being tempted.

Hebrews 2:18

Sometimes temptation to do wrong is so strong and the pressure is so intense from other guys that it's hard to fight it off. Have you ever wanted to shout, "God, You don't know what it's like down here!"? You could shout that at Him but you would be wrong.

Jesus faced every kind of temptation you will ever have to face and He never gave in. Are you thinking, "Yeah, but He is God"? Yes, He is, that's why it's so cool that He wants to help you fight temptation. You can stand up against it using His strength. Pretty cool, huh?

ChallengePoint

Temptations come. There's no way around it. Sometimes a friend will tempt you to steal something or to rip up another guy's reputation or to push some new kid out to the fringe so he has no friends. Temptation comes, but if you turn to God for help you can fight it off. He loves you and promises to be there for you.

Witnessing His Power

There are things about Him that people cannot see – His eternal power and all the things that make Him God. But since the beginning of the world those things have been easy to understand by what God has made. So people have no excuse for the bad things they do.

Romans 1:20

Evidence. A detective searches for evidence to answer questions and solve mysteries. The evidence is examined and conclusions are drawn from it. If you needed to prove God's power to someone, where would you begin?

There's plenty of evidence of His power in the world around you. Look at the sun, moon and zillions of stars in the sky. Look at the mountains and oceans. God's creations show God's power and leave no doubt that He is forever.

ChallengePoint

Understanding God's power is important because it gives you something to hold on to when the world goes crazy. The news is filled with reports of wars and murders. There are terrible natural disasters. The world can be a scary place, so you need to know that God's power is greater than anything else. His power is there for you. He loves you.

Having Faith

Faith means being sure of the things we hope for and knowing that something is real even if we do not see it.

Hebrews 11:1

Magicians and illusionists do amazing tricks to try to make their audience believe they see things that aren't really true. Some illusionists are so courageous that they do things like making the Statue of Liberty disappear.

God is not an illusionist. He is honest and powerful. What the Bible tells you about God and His work is absolutely true. When you know Him and trust Him you can have faith in everything the Bible tells you about Him. Even though you can't see God, you can have faith in Him.

ChallengePoint

Faith is believing and trusting, even if you can't see something. You can have faith in God and in what the Bible tells you about Him. What God says about Himself in the Bible is the absolute truth. He never lies or pads the truth. You can believe it.

"I tell you the truth," Jesus said, "this poor widow has given more than all the rest of them. For they have given a tiny part of their surplus, but she, poor as she is, has given everything she has."

Luke 21:3-4

God wants ... everything. In this Scripture verse, Jesus is commenting on a woman who gave all the money she had to God's work. She didn't just give a little or split it 50-50 with Him. She gave it all.

That kind of devotion is exactly what God wants from you. OK, maybe you don't have a lot of money to give. This Scripture verse doesn't even mean that you give every cent to God. It means that you give your whole heart – complete love and devotion to Him. When you do that then your money will be used in the way God wants.

ChallengePoint

Don't hold back from God. That means don't think you can be God's guy on Sunday but on Tuesday you can do whatever you want. Give your whole heart to God, every day. Exciting things will happen for you then!

Knowing God by

Suppressing Our Pride

March 6

"Be careful! When you do good things, don't do them in front of people to be seen by them. If you do that, you will have no reward from your Father in heaven."

Matthew 6:1

Most people like attention, especially if they do something good. They want people to notice and pat them on the back or make a big deal about how kind or generous or helpful they are. If they can get some kind of award for their good deed, that's even better.

Whoa. That's not God's way. God doesn't want you to do good deeds to get praise from other people. He wants you to do nice things for others because you love Him and you love others. That requires a pureness in your heart that God will see as your motivation. Now, God is serious about this. People who do good deeds just for praise will only get praise from others – not from God.

ChallengePoint

Does this sound extreme to you? Well, God doesn't mess around. He wants your motivation to be right – obeying Him, loving Him and loving others. If your motivation for what you do comes from anywhere else … you are toast. Don't count on any reward from Him.

Trusting in Him

Trusting unfaithful people when you are in trouble is like eating with a broken tooth or walking with a crippled foot.

Proverbs 25:19

You're ready to run in a big race ... really big. And more than ANYTHING, you want to win this race because your biggest competitor is running too. He has beaten you the last four times you raced and you WANT to win this one. So you train and eat right to get ready for this race. Then, the day before the race you take a tumble down the stairs and sprain your ankle. It immediately swells up like a watermelon and hurts even when you breathe, let alone when you walk on it. Whew. What are your chances of winning that race now? Not so good, eh?

Trusting someone who isn't dependable is much the same as trusting your bad ankle in a race. You will end up falling on your face. People are never as dependable as God is, and unreliable people are the worst! Hey, there is an easy answer to this ... trust God.

ChallengePoint

It's OK to have friends who give you advice. It's even good to talk things through with others when you have trouble. But never trust anyone more than you trust God. He's the One you can depend on ... always.

Using His Gifts

God can give you more blessings than you need. Then you will always have plenty of everything – enough to give to every good work. It is written in the Scriptures: "He gives freely to the poor. The things He does are right and will continue forever."

2 Corinthians 9:8-9

God gives you a lot. Stop and think about it. Don't get hung up on the idea that some of the "stuff" you have came from your parents, your friends or even because you worked for it. Those are sidebar things. EVERYTHING you have comes from God ultimately. After all, He made everything there is.

Maybe you've been super-blessed and you have a very comfortable life, or maybe your family just barely scrapes by every month. Regardless of what you have, share it. Yep, He gives you what you need and wants you to share with others so they have what they need too.

ChallengePoint

No one is alone in this world. God instructs His children to help one another and look out for one another. Whatever you have – however much you have – find someone to share it with.

> *"Teach these new disciples to obey all the commands I have given you. And be sure of this: I am with you always, even to the end of the age."*
>
> *Matthew 28:20*

Sometimes life stinks. Sometimes people hurt you. Sometimes families break up and one parent or the other leaves. Sometimes friends stop being friends. Sometimes when the going gets tough ... people leave.

One of the ways you can know God loves you totally is that He will never, ever leave you. Never. He promises. His love is so strong that He will stick with you no matter how tough life gets; regardless of whether you are loving Him back or not. He wants you to obey Him and do His work, of course. But even if sometimes you don't ... He doesn't leave you.

ChallengePoint

When you think about it, God's promise to be with you always is pretty motivating to love Him, isn't it? Seriously, if He loves you that much and promises to stick close to you ... how can you do anything but love Him back?

Praying

"If My people, who are called by My name, will humble themselves and pray and seek My face and turn from their wicked ways, then will I hear from heaven and will forgive their sin and will heal their land."

2 Chronicles 7:14

Of course, you would never do this – but maybe you've seen a two-year-old throw a raging temper tantrum in a store. His mom or dad won't buy him something so he throws himself on the floor, screaming ... like that will change his parents' mind. Yeah, right.

Guess what, it doesn't work with God either. But God promises to hear your prayers and to answer them according to His will. Look at the characteristics of the praying person given in this verse: humbleness (that means not demanding your way), seeking God's face (that means listening for what He wants), turning from wicked ways (wow, that means a lot of things, like not being selfish).

ChallengePoint

Are the three characteristics given in this verse true of you? Or are you sometimes like a tantrum-throwing two-year-old? God wants to answer your prayers. Do your part and approach Him with the love He deserves.

Seeking His Protection

"God blesses those people who grieve. They will find comfort!"

Matthew 5:4

When you think about protection you probably think of someone keeping you safe in a storm. Maybe you think of your protector as someone who stops a bully from beating you up. Those are certainly kinds of protection.

Have you ever thought that you need protection when you're mourning? Weird, huh? It's true though. When you are grieving because someone you loved has died or moved away, your resistance is down. That's a perfect time for Satan to creep into your heart and set up residence.

Turn to God for comfort and He will protect your tender heart. He will comfort you and keep Satan far away while your grief heals.

ChallengePoint

It always comes back to two things: (1) God loves you. (2) He's always there for you. That doesn't mean that life will always be easy or that you will never hurt. It just means that He will protect you through whatever pain life brings.

Serving Him

"Good people bring good things out of their hearts, but evil people bring evil things out of their hearts."

Matthew 12:35

The thing about serving God is that you can't just do it any old way. There's not really any way to serve God by hurting someone or cheating others. That's bad stuff that doesn't honor God. The flip side of this is that God can be served by the good things you do. From where do those good things come? From a healthy heart that honors and serves God.

God wants your service, and He will help keep your heart obedient and healthy. He will give you strength to resist saying mean things and playing unfairly. He will help you learn to love those around you.

ChallengePoint

If you fill a pitcher with water, when you pour the liquid into a glass, you don't expect to have a glass of chocolate milk, do you? Nope, what's in the pitcher is what comes out. In that same way, what's in your heart will come out in the way you live. If your heart is healthy and filled with love and kindness, that's what will come out. Serve God from a healthy heart.

Obeying Him

Wisdom begins with respect for the LORD; those who obey His orders have good understanding. He should be praised forever.

Psalm 111:10

Do you know someone who thinks he is always right? Some guys think the only way to do things is their way. This kind of guy is a know-it-all. He thinks he is the smartest guy ever. But he isn't.

This Scripture verse states that real smarts comes from obeying God. True respect for God is where obedience begins. But to obey God's commandments you have to know them, and that means reading His Word – the Bible. A truly smart person knows God's commandments and obeys them. By doing that a person gets smarter and smarter!

ChallengePoint

If you're going to be obedient, you have to know what is right and wrong. Reading God's Word is the best place to learn that. Study God's word and obey the commandments you find there. Then you will be wise and will grow wiser each day.

Obeying Him

If you obey every law except one, you are still guilty of breaking them all.

James 2:10

Hey, you're not so bad, right? After all, you have never murdered anyone or robbed a bank, right? So when it comes to the whole obeying God thing, you feel like you're doing pretty well. There are guys who are a lot worse than you, right? Right.

Well, here's the deal – even if you only break ONE of God's laws, in God's eyes, you might as well have broken all of them. Why does the Bible say that? Because God wants complete obedience from His children. He doesn't put up with attempts to justify away one little bit of disobedience. Nope, God wants complete obedience.

ChallengePoint

Is this news to you? Did you think you were doing OK by just obeying the easy stuff? It's good to obey as much as you can, but never be satisfied with just being pretty good. Keep learning and growing and obeying more and more.

"Even if that person wrongs you seven times a day and each time turns again and asks forgiveness, you must forgive."

Luke 17:4

A friend cheats when you're playing a game with him. You get mad and stop playing. He apologizes; you forgive him and start a new game. What if this pattern happens over and over? How many times do you have to put up with it? A lot more than you probably want to – even seven times a day! Why? Why would God ask you to be so forgiving and patient? Because He is.

Stop and think about how many times God has to forgive you. Seriously, how many times a day do you have unkind thoughts? What about feelings of pride? How often do you talk back to your mom or complain about rules? Now, how often does God forgive you for those things? Do you know the answer to that? Every single time.

ChallengePoint

God is a forgiving God because He loves you. When you ask for His forgiveness, He will give it every time – even seven times a day. Pass that same forgiving spirit along to others and forgive them. It's God's way.

Seeking His Guidance

"I will instruct you and teach you in the way you should go; I will counsel you and watch over you."

Psalm 32:8

Have you ever gone through a maze? You know what that is, right? Sometimes they are made in cornfields. The corn is cut so that you can go rushing down one cleared aisle, thinking you are heading out of the cornfield, but then you come to a dead end. You turn and rush the other way and on and on. It takes a while and several mistakes before you finally find your way out.

Life feels like that sometimes. You rush to do one thing, then find out that's probably not right for you, so you rush in another direction. It's no fun. It's also not necessary. God has promised to guide you. He knows what's best for you because He can see the big picture from when you were in diapers all the way to the end of your life. Ask God for guidance. He will give it.

ChallengePoint

Why put yourself through the agony of running one way and then another? God already has a plan for your life and you know it's a good one since He loves you so much. Stop running around and just ask Him to guide you.

His Faithfulness

I am certain that God, who began the good work within you, will continue His work until it is finally finished on the day when Christ Jesus returns.

Philippians 1:6

Some years ago superglue was invented. This glue is so strong and works so quickly that before long hospital emergency rooms were treating patients who had accidentally glued their fingers together. It's nearly impossible to break the bond of superglue.

That stick-to-it-ive-ness is nothing compared to God. From the minute you asked Jesus into your heart, God started working in you. He started teaching you and guiding you in how to live for Him and be a good example to those around you. He will keep right on doing that till you go to heaven. He is faithful and sticks closer to you than superglued fingers do to each other!

ChallengePoint

Wow. Think about how much God loves you. He sticks close to you – forever. He keeps teaching you and training you and, more than anything else, loving you. How cool is that?

Enduring

Your words came to me, and I listened carefully to them.
Your words made me very happy, because I am called by
Your name, LORD God All-Powerful.

Jeremiah 15:16

What's your favorite food? If its pizza, chips, hot dogs or ice cream, you probably get a fairly steady lecture from your mom or dad about eating healthy food so your body gets the fuel it needs to keep going. Junk food doesn't give your body that fuel. It might give a jump start, but it doesn't last. You couldn't run a marathon after filling up on ice cream. You wouldn't have enough endurance.

Have you ever thought about the fact that your heart and soul are the same way? To be able to stand strong for God you've got to feed your soul healthy food, and that comes from God's Word. Read the Bible. Memorize it so it's tucked away in your heart. You'll never be sorry.

ChallengePoint

There are constant temptations to turn away from God; subtle things that don't seem to matter a lot ... except they do because they open the door to more things that are disobedient to God's will. The only way to endure, is to read and learn God's Word. Let it sink into your heart.

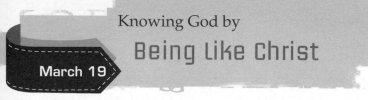

Knowing God by
Being Like Christ

March 19

The LORD hates every liar, but He is the friend of all who can be trusted.

Proverbs 12:22

Be like Christ ... be like Christ. Wow, that's a big order, isn't it? Come on, Christ was God! He was perfect, so how could you possibly be like Him? Yes, it is a big order. But you can take it in steps. For example, as this verse tells you ... don't lie. Christ was always truthful (kind, but truthful).

Read through the Gospels – you won't find Him saying what He thinks people want to hear. He was honest. So take one small step to being Christlike by being truthful. Honesty pleases God and it's the fairest thing for other people too.

ChallengePoint

It's hard to be truthful sometimes because you want people to like you, right? It's easiest to just tell them what you know they want to hear instead of saying what you're really thinking. Stop it. Be courageous – be honest. It's the Jesus way.

Being Like Christ

Not that I was ever in need, for I have learned how to be content with whatever I have.

Philippians 4:11

How much of your time do you spend thinking about the stuff you want? Stuff like video game systems, expensive basketball shoes, fishing rods ... or whatever your "thing" is. Everyone fights "Give it to me" thoughts at some point in their lives because we live in a world that puts a lot of importance on stuff. Most of the world feels that the people with the most stuff are the winners in life.

God doesn't agree. Becoming more like Christ means finding that place of peace in your life where you're happy where you are and with what you've got. The main reason you can find that peaceful place – is because you know you have God – and He is enough.

ChallengePoint

This kind of peace is a tough thing to find because everything from television, magazines, and even your friends, are bombarding you with the pressure to get more stuff. Having more stuff is a status symbol in this world. But it isn't a sign of success with God. In fact, success as far as God's concerned is contentment and peace with what you have. Can you find that?

Two people are better than one, because they get more done by working together. If one falls down, the other can help him up. But it is bad for the person who is alone and falls, because no one is there to help.

Ecclesiastes 4:9-10

Who's your best buddy? Why is he such a good friend? What kinds of things do you guys enjoy doing together? You probably like the same things and have the same sense of humor, right? When you need help, who do you call? When you want to have fun, who do you call? When someone is picking on you, who stands up for you? Yep, that's your buddy.

What a great idea God had to give you friends. Did you ever think about that? Your best buddy is a gift from God. What's more, that buddy is evidence of God's love for you. God knew you wouldn't want to be alone. He knew there would be times when you needed a friend. He knew life would be more fun with friends. He knew you could be stronger with a friend by your side.

ChallengePoint

Thank God right now for your friends ... especially your best friend. He is God's gift to you. Because God loves you He gave you people in your life to have fun with.

We love because He first loved us.

1 John 4:19

Have you heard of "pay it forward"? You see the concept in TV commercials sometimes – one person does something unexpectedly kind for someone else. Then, that person does something nice for another person who is then kind to yet another person. One person's kind act causes a chain reaction of kindness.

That's how God's love seems to affect people. When one person actually understands how much God loves him (and even how unworthy he is of that love) then he shows love to a person in his life. It's like setting up rows of dominoes and then knocking over the first one, which hits the next, which hits the next ... until they all fall. God's love is contagious. When you get a glimpse of the truth that He loves you so completely, you can't help but pass it on to others.

ChallengePoint

Some people say that the way God's children live on this earth may be the only way that some people ever get a glimpse of His love. Some people won't go to church. They won't read the Bible. But they can still see God's love – through you.

Showing Courage

"I give you peace, the kind of peace that only I can give. It isn't like the peace that this world can give. So don't be worried or afraid."

John 14:27

Guys are supposed to be tough, right? It's not cool to admit when you're afraid. Some guys put on a macho, tough guy front, but on the inside they are terrified. They may try to find some kind of peace of mind through the friends they hang out with or how they treat others (usually not very nice). Whatever ... it won't work.

The ability to actually be courageous comes only when you have peace about who is in control of your life. When you know that God is running things, you can have peace of mind and heart, regardless of what's going on around you.

ChallengePoint

People who don't know God won't understand this kind of peace. But it's the best kind. You don't have to worry. You don't have to be afraid. Just let God watch over you and you can be at peace.

Witnessing His Power

March 24

> *"You will receive power when the Holy Spirit comes upon you. And you will be My witnesses, telling people about Me everywhere – in Jerusalem, throughout Judea, in Samaria, and to the ends of the earth."*
>
> *Acts 1:8*

God's power created the sun, the stars, the moon, the whole world and everything in it. God's power raised Jesus back to life. God's power comes to you through the presence of the Holy Spirit in you.

Is that kind of a hard concept to understand? That's because the Holy Spirit is a ... Spirit. God's Spirit comes to live in your heart and gives you power to do the work God has chosen for you to do. Pretty cool, huh?

You don't have to worry about how you're going to have the strength or energy to do what God wants because it comes from Him!

ChallengePoint

If you've asked Jesus into your heart, God's Spirit is living in you right now. That means His power is there for you. When you need help or strength or courage, just ask God for it. Then, let His Spirit guide you.

His Love

March 25

"The greatest love a person can show is to die for his friends."

John 15:13

How far would you go to help a buddy? Most people will do what they can to help someone else as long as it doesn't cost them anything. People seem to have an internal standard that is their guide for how much time they will spend helping someone else. It also guides how much energy they will give and how much money they will spend. In other words, there is a cut-off point for their love actions.

God doesn't have a cut-off point. His love for you is so great that He sent Jesus (His only Son) to earth. Jesus held nothing back – He died for you. That's total and complete love.

ChallengePoint

God's love for you is complete. He holds nothing back. How does your love for Him measure up? Do you hold some parts of your life back from Him or have you given Him your whole heart?

Knowing God by

Praying

Never give up praying. And when you pray, keep alert and be thankful.

Colossians 4:2

Do you pray? Do you pray even when you aren't in trouble? Ok, maybe you say prayers while you're falling asleep at night. But does your mind stay alert when you are praying then? Alert like you're listening for God's voice? He will guide you in what to pray about. He will bring people to mind who need your prayers.

An alert mind is important. A thankful heart is also important because that means you recognize all that God does for you.

ChallengePoint

Don't make your prayer life half-hearted. Devote yourself to prayer. Believe that God will answer. Constant prayer will help you get to know God better and you will be able to see Him working in your life.

Seeking His Protection

Jesus said, "Come to Me, all of you who are weary and carry heavy burdens, and I will give you rest."

Matthew 11:28

Here's the usual cycle:

- You have a problem at school or at home.
- You come up with a plan to solve the problem.
- You work hard at your plan.
- You work harder.
- You work even harder.
- You get really tired.
- You want to give up.

So ... what do you do? Jesus has the answer. He cares about your problems. He knows life gets pretty tough sometimes – He promises to help.

ChallengePoint

Jesus promises rest from the problems and stresses of life. All you have to do is come to Him. Ask Him for help and trust that He'll give it.

Serving Him

Jesus said, "Come follow Me, and I will make you fish for people." So Simon and Andrew immediately left their nets and followed Him.

Matthew 4:19-20

Jesus made this statement to men who earned their living by fishing ... for fish. He was asking them to leave their jobs; their only means of earning money, to follow Him around the countryside, listening to Him teach and learning by watching what He did.

In the process, they would learn how to teach people about God, so they would be fishing for people in order to bring people to a place where they understood who God is and how much He loves them.

ChallengePoint

Serving God begins with following Him. Ask God to show you how you can serve Him. God's desire is for all people to love and follow Him and that must begin with people first hearing about God's love. That's fishing for people!

Just as each of us has one body with many members, and these members do not all have the same function, so in Christ we who are many form one body, and each member belongs to all the others.

Romans 12:4-5

Can you throw a ball with your foot? How about play a piano with your nose? That's silly talk, isn't it? But it makes you stop and think about how each part of your body has a specific job. From your listening ears to your tapping toes to your digesting stomach, each part of your body has a specific job to do.

It's the same with God's body, which you are a member of. Some members of God's body have the job of teaching. Some to encourage others. Some are good at sharing their faith with others. You see, each person has a job to do for God, as part of His family. No person's job is more important than another, it's just different.

ChallengePoint

What is your favorite thing to do? The way you can serve God is probably related to that. Maybe you're good at making friends, maybe you're good at listening to others, or teaching or sports or music. Whatever you're good at, you can serve God by doing that thing.

Obeying Him

> *"You are the salt of the earth. But what good is salt if it has lost its flavor? Can you make it salty again? It will be thrown out and trampled underfoot as worthless."*
>
> Matthew 5:13

Salt has a job to do. It's flavorful. You probably enjoy its flavor on chips, popcorn or pretzels. It is also used as a preservative to make foods last longer. If something happens to the salt and it doesn't do its job anymore, it's pretty much useless.

Why does Jesus use the example of salt in this verse? He's talking about Christians who are obeying God and serving Him. Christians who are taking a stand for Him. When a person stops doing that, then he isn't doing his job and his purpose is gone. God doesn't accept half-hearted obedience. He wants your full heart obeying Him all the time. Otherwise, you are like flavorless salt.

ChallengePoint

You know what to do ... obey God. How terrible it would be to know that you've disappointed God by not obeying and serving Him. It could happen ... but it's up to you.

If we say we have not sinned, we make God a liar, and we do not accept God's teaching.

1 John 1:10

The thing about God is that you can't bluff around Him, you can't fool Him, so you might as well not lie to Him. You can say to other people that you don't do anything wrong. You can even give excuses about why the choices you make and the things you do are OK ... but God knows the truth.

He insists on obedience, and if you try to fake that obedience, then you are just insulting Him. You're also showing that your claims to love Him and to want to obey Him are only half-hearted.

ChallengePoint

Don't bother trying to fool God. Just be honest with Him. Come clean when you mess up – admit it and confess it. He wants your obedience, but He will forgive you when you confess. That wipes the slate clean and you can start over.

Say what you mean,
mean what you say,
but don't say it mean.
– Anonymous

April

Obeying Him

"What can a man give in exchange for his soul?"

Mark 8:37

You get to choose – is it more important to you to obey God or to hang out with a bunch of guys who do their own thing, with no concern at all for God or His commandments?

Stop – don't give the answer you *think* you are supposed to give. Be honest. After all, no one but you and God have to know the truth. OK, are you ready? If your honest-from-the-heart-answer is that you'd rather hang out with the guys but you'd kind of like God to be happy with you too ... tough luck.

Here's the deal – God doesn't mess around with the obedience thing. Being a child of God means obeying Him and that begins with asking Jesus to be your Savior. If hangin' with the guys is more important to you than that, then yeah, you will lose your chance of eternal life.

ChallengePoint

Is hangin' with the guys more important than heaven? Really? Come on, look at the big picture of eternity with God. The here and now will very quickly be the day that "used to be" and there are more important things. Don't give up your soul for what seems like fun today.

Anyone who knows the right thing to do, but does not do it, is sinning.

James 4:17

Here's the situation: A new kid comes to your school. Mr. Big Shot in your class decides he doesn't like the new kid, so he makes fun of him and picks on him all the time. Other guys follow the lead of Mr. Big Shot and do the same. Poor new kid never had a chance. You join in the abuse of the new kid too, even though you know it really isn't the right thing to do. But hey, it's no big deal 'cause everyone is doing it.

Sorry, dude, but you are totally and completely wrong. God says if you know the right thing to do and choose not to do it ... it's a sin. Plain and simple.

ChallengePoint

You see, obedience is very important to God. He doesn't mess around with it. Don't try to fake it – you may fool other people, but God knows. When you know deep in your heart that God disapproves of something and you do it anyway – it's sin.

Confessing Sin

April 3

People who conceal their sins will not prosper, but if they confess and turn from them, they will receive mercy.

Proverbs 28:13

There's an old saying that goes, "You can fool all of the people some of the time, and some of the people all of the time. But you can't fool all of the people all of the time." Here's an addition to that: "You can't fool God ANY of the time."

That bears true in this verse. Whatever you choose to do in secret may be secret from other people – hidden sin – but God knows about it. So your disobedience will be punished. There's only one way out of that mess ... confess your sins and God will forgive you.

ChallengePoint

Confession cleans up your relationship with God. Your sin puts up a barrier between you and God. Confessing your sin tears it down and makes your relationship healthy again.

Knowing God by

Seeking His Guidance

All Scripture is God-breathed and is useful for teaching,
rebuking, correcting and training in righteousness.

2 Timothy 3:16

Some things you buy have "Some assembly required"
stamped on the box. The easiest way to put your new
purchase together is to read the step-by-step instructions.
However, some people choose to ignore the instructions
and figure things out on their own. Sometimes that works
out fine, but sometimes it causes big problems.

Think about the Christian life for a minute. If you're
going to do it right, it would help to have an instruction
manual, right? Well ... you do. It's called the Bible, and
God put pretty much everything in it that you need to
know.

ChallengePoint

If God's guidance and instruction come from the Bible,
then it would make a lot of sense to read it, right? Yep,
that's the key ... read His Word.

Understanding Anger

Love isn't selfish or quick tempered. It doesn't keep a record of wrongs that others do.

1 Corinthians 13:5

There's a chain of info that's the background of this verse. Here's how it goes:

- God said to love others. It's such an important command that Jesus said it's the second most important one.
- Info in 1 Corinthians 13 gives a description of how honest-to-goodness love acts.
- Love doesn't focus on anger. It doesn't insist on always having its way.
- God guides His children away from anger and toward love.

ChallengePoint

Come on, everyone gets angry sometimes. But if a person is focusing his heart on loving others (as God says to do) anger will not be the norm and when anger happens, it will go away quickly.

His Faithfulness

"Earth and sky will be destroyed, but the words I have said will never be destroyed."

Mark 13:31

God will never disappear. His Word, the Bible, will never disappear. Oh sure, the leather-bound paper-filled books may wear out and be gone, but His words will always live in the hearts of His children.

Do you believe that God's words are forever? He says it's true. If you're not paying much attention to your Bible; if it's lying in the corner underneath your baseball glove – then you're not living as though you believe it. Faithfulness means forever and God says His words will be around forever.

ChallengePoint

If God's Word is going to last forever then it must be important. So make time every day to read His Word. Think about it and let it settle in your mind and heart.

Seeking Salvation

Everyone who calls on the name of the LORD will be saved.

Joel 2:32

Some clubs require a lot of stuff from guys who want to join. They might make guys do dangerous or dumb things. They might ask guys to eat weird foods or wear weird-looking clothes. It's a long process to become a member of some teams.

Is it a lot of work to become a member of God's family? Does God make you do a lot of things like a club might? Nope. All you have to do to become a member of God's family and be saved is ... ask. God's plan was that Jesus came to earth, died for your sins, came back to life and now lives in heaven again with God, the Father. All you have to do is call on His name to be saved. Pretty easy, right?

ChallengePoint

God made the plan for salvation as easy as possible. Have you done it? Call on Jesus and the power of His name. Confess your sins and ask Him to live in your heart. You are then saved into His family.

Being Thankful

Give thanks to the LORD, for He is good; His love endures forever.

1 Chronicles 16:34

Say thanks. Simple enough, right? But how often do you do it? Maybe you don't get why it's so important. God knows He is all-powerful, so why does He need you to say thanks?

Because when you take the time to think about what you're thankful for, you're thinking about God. That helps your faith grow stronger and helps you appreciate God more. Saying thanks is so easy, but doing it brings a lot of good things for you.

ChallengePoint

Thankfulness helps you get to know God better, because as you think about what you are thankful for, you are appreciating God and all He does for you. What a happy thing. Take time every day to thank God for at least one thing He did for you.

Celebrating Him

April 9

It is wonderful each morning to tell about Your love and at night to announce how faithful You are.

Psalm 92:2

God loves you ... no matter what. No matter how many goofy or dumb things you do or how many times you ignore Him or disappoint Him ... He just keeps on loving you.

That's worth celebrating, right? God is faithful too. That means He keeps His promises, always and always. He means what He says. He says what He means. He does what He says. He is faithful.

ChallengePoint

God loves you no matter what. He is always faithful. Those two things are worth celebrating. Throw a party! Sing a song! Celebrate how awesome God is!

Knowing God by

Enduring

And you, my son Solomon, acknowledge the God of your father, and serve Him with wholehearted devotion and with a willing mind, for the LORD searches every heart and understands every motive behind the thoughts. If you seek Him, He will be found by you; but if you forsake Him, He will reject you forever.

1 Chronicles 28:9

The easy way is not always the best way." Have you heard that before? Maybe one of your parents or teachers has encouraged you to work hard for something. It means working hard through problems. It means working hard even if you're injured, tired or stressed.

That's endurance. It takes your whole heart and mind, and it means you can't fake your way through. God sees your heart. He knows the real you.

ChallengePoint

Endurance. Work hard, be strong, give it your all. It's worth it to know God with your whole heart and mind.

"Do to others whatever you would like them to do to you. This is the essence of all that is taught in the law and the prophets."

Matthew 7:12

Do you feel that it's OK to tell lies about someone else – lies that make them look bad and you look good? Do you feel like you deserve to look important – more important than other guys? OK, then how do you feel if that same guy tells a lie about you? Yeah, that's not fun, is it?

Living like Christ means treating others with respect, honesty and love. That's how you'd like to be treated, right? Christ even treated His enemies that way. He understood how to disagree with others in a respectful way. Christ said that loving others is the second most important commandment.

ChallengePoint

Loving others isn't always easy. But a reminder to treat others the way you would like to be treated is always good. The first step to treating others the way Christ did is to treat them the way you would like to be treated yourself.

Being Like Christ

Do not be interested only in your own life, but be interested in the lives of others.

Philippians 2:4

Here's a news flash ... life isn't all about you. It's hard to not look at everything that happens and think about how it affects you or how it makes you look. But to live like Christ you have to make your brain think in a different way. You have to take a different track.

Sometimes you need to look at things and think about how other people are affected. Celebrate with them when they have good news (even if it's not good news for you) and sympathize with them when they have sad news (even if it's great news for you.) Is this easy? Nope. Is it important? Yep.

ChallengePoint

Think about life with this kind of priority in mind: Jesus first, others next, yourself last. You'll be living like Christ if you put others' needs and concerns before your own.

Loving Others

"Love your enemies! Do good to them. Lend to them without expecting to be repaid. Then your reward from heaven will be very great, and you will truly be acting as children of the Most High', for He is kind to those who are unthankful and wicked."

Luke 6:35

1. Love God. (OK, done. That's an easy one.)
2. Love others. (Done. After all, it's easy to love your friends.)
3. Love your enemies. (Whoa. Love your enemies? Right. You'd probably rather pound them. BIFF! BANG! POW!)

You can't do that if you're going to love the way God loves.

ChallengePoint

Think about this ... God loves those who are unthankful and wicked ... sometimes that is YOU. Now, aren't you glad He loves that way? Can you learn from Him and love that way too?

Loving Others

Love is patient and kind. Love is not jealous, it does not brag, and it is not proud.

1 Corinthians 13:4

When a person gets a job, he is given a job description. That's how he knows what is expected of him. It gives a measurement of how well the worker is doing. God did a cool thing in 1 Corinthians 13. He gave a sort of job description for love. It's really helpful since the Bible is filled with the command to love others.

This verse alone tells you two things love is: patient and kind. It also tells you three things love isn't: jealous, boastful or proud. So here are ways to measure your emotions about someone to find out if you're really being loving or not.

ChallengePoint

Loving others is really important to God. He says it a lot in the Bible. It helps to have the job description in 1 Corinthians 13. It is a place to begin to measure your emotions and see how you're doing in the "loving others department."

Knowing God by
Showing Courage

So be strong and courageous! Do not be afraid and do not panic before them. For the LORD your God will personally go ahead of you. He will neither fail you nor abandon you.

Deuteronomy 31:6

Sometimes the scariest thing is feeling like you're alone. Whatever task is before you; whatever job you have; you don't have the sense that anyone is helping you. You feel like you have to figure things out by yourself and come up with a plan alone.

Take courage from this: YOU ARE NOT ALONE. God promised to stick close to you. Even better, He says He will go before you. So you know that whatever happens, He knew about it first. No worries then!

ChallengePoint

Courage can come from the absolute certainty that God is always with you and that nothing surprises Him. He knows what's going to happen in your life before it even happens. He's already got a plan laid out.

We can win with God's help. He will defeat our enemies.

Psalm 60:12

No worries. Nothing to fear. The God on your side is bigger and more powerful than anything else. Just like a running back on a football team, with a blocker clearing out the opposing players as he runs down the field, you have the most powerful, awesome blocker clearing the way for you – God.

His power will smash His enemies, who, by the way, are your enemies too. His amazing power is fighting for you, protecting you and guiding you!

ChallengePoint

Knowing that God is on your side and that His amazing power is fighting for you and protecting you should give you great peace. You've got nothing to fear, just trust God. Tell Him what's going on and look for His power protecting and guiding you.

Having Faith

What good is it, dear brothers and sisters, if you say you have faith but don't show it by your actions? Can that kind of faith save anyone?

James 2:14

Lip service is what you give when you say all the right things, but your actions don't back up what you say. You may say Christian things. You may know Bible verses and go to church every week, but if your life doesn't show love and concern for others, then all your Christian words are just a waste of good air.

Faith is more than knowing how to say the right words. Faith shows in the way you live – concern for others and a desire to love and help them.

ChallengePoint

Put your faith to work. Do the work God wants you to do. Don't just talk about it … do it.

Knowing God by
Giving

*By everything I did, I showed how you should work to help
everyone who is weak. Remember that our Lord Jesus said,
"More blessings come from giving than from receiving."*

Acts 20:35

You've seen the pictures of kids in other parts of the
world who don't have food to eat. Many of them don't
have homes to live in. The idea of them having video
games, cell phones, or TVs to watch is ridiculous.

People who don't know where their next meal is
coming from don't worry about that kind of stuff. So
what? What should this mean to you? What God has
given you should be shared with those who have needs.

ChallengePoint

It feels good to help someone. Giving doesn't always
mean giving money. Sometimes you can help others by
giving time and helping them with something. Show your
love for God by giving.

"Why do you look at the speck of sawdust in your brother's eye and pay no attention to the plank in your own eye?"

Matthew 7:3

Pride is a strange thing. It blinds you to your own faults and problems. Pride puffs you up like a blowfish until you think you are totally awesome and amazing.

However, the flip side of pride is that it looks at others and sees only their problems and faults. After all, it makes you feel better about yourself if you compare yourself to someone who is messing up or failing all the time. Pride doesn't fool God.

ChallengePoint

Criticizing others while ignoring or covering up your own problems is not smart. Take care of your own problems. Ask God to help you focus on being more obedient to Him and more loving to others. Take care of yourself and let others take care of themselves.

Knowing God by
Abiding in Him

"Be still and know that I am God! I will be honored by every nation. I will be honored throughout the world."

Psalm 46:10

Think about your family. You probably know the people in your family better than you know anyone else. Why? Because you spend time with them. You know what each of them likes. You know what each of them doesn't like.

You know what the rules of the family are and what the jobs of the family are. You know them. OK, switch that over to God. How can you know Him better and better? Spend time with Him.

ChallengePoint

Hanging out with God is called "abiding." It means being really close to Him; being quiet and listening for Him to speak in your heart. It's the way to know Him. Make time in your life to be in a quiet place, be still and think about God. He will speak in your heart.

Trusting Him

It is better to trust the Lord than to trust people.

Psalm 118:8

Let's say you are camping in the woods and a heavy rainstorm begins. You rush into your tent, close the flap door and settle in to wait for the storm to end. But after a few minutes, your tent begins to leak in one spot; then in another and another. Pretty soon you are as wet as you would be if you sat outside. Turns out, your tent wasn't such a safe place to go.

A refuge ... a safe place to hide ... needs to be a place where you will be safe ... no matter what. God is the safest place. Some people put their trust in people instead of God. But people fail sometimes. They make mistakes. They disappoint us.

ChallengePoint

God is always the same. He is strong, powerful and loves you more than you can imagine. Putting your trust in Him is the safest and best choice. You can always count on God.

I sing to the Lord because He has taken care of me.

Psalm 13:6

Do you like to sing? Are you good at it? Some people love to sing and they do so loudly, but, um, they aren't so good at it. Maybe you aren't such a great singer, but you are probably good at something else.

God gives each of His children talents and abilities and He loves it when they use those things to serve Him or praise Him. Don't get hung up on whether you are the "best" at whatever you do; just do what you can with joy and praise in your heart to God, who made it all possible.

ChallengePoint

Sing, dance, write, be a friend, be a helper ... gifts and abilities come in lots of different forms. Recognize what you're good at and use it to serve God!

But the LORD said to Samuel, "Don't look at how handsome Eliab is or how tall he is, because I have not chosen him. God does not see the same way people see. People look at the outside of a person, but the LORD looks at the heart."

1 Samuel 16:7

The way our world works it appears that the tallest, handsomest guys get the most respect. The athletes, movie stars or richest guys become heroes to everyone else.

That's dumb. God doesn't care what a person looks like on the outside. He judges a person's worth by what's going on in his heart. If a guy's heart is focused on serving God, then he is a success in God's eyes.

ChallengePoint

God's love focuses on your heart. How is your heart doing? Does it want to serve God? Does it love Him? Is God the most important Person in your life? He loves you lots and He doesn't get hung up on how you look, like people do. God just loves YOU. Pretty cool, huh?

If any of you need wisdom, you should ask God, and it will be given to you. God is generous and won't correct you for asking.

James 1:5

If you're like most guys, you know how to measure when it's a good time to ask your mom or dad for something, and when it might be best to keep your mouth shut. There are just some moods or stresses that you can be sure will lead to a "No" whatever you ask.

Here's a cool thing about God – He doesn't have bad moods or times when He's too busy to listen to your requests. He is always ready to listen and always ready to answer. He never gets annoyed at your requests. This doesn't mean that He will always do what you ask Him to do or change what you want changed. He knows what's best for you. But He *will* always listen.

ChallengePoint

God sees the big picture of your whole life and the lives of those around you. He will hear your requests and prayers. He may not do what you think He should, but He does what's best for you in the long run. Ask Him whatever you want, tell Him your requests. Trust His answer.

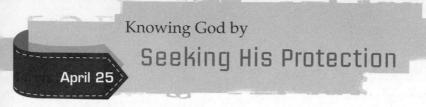

Knowing God by
Seeking His Protection

The LORD gives His people strength. The LORD blesses them with peace.

Psalm 29:11

When you think about God protecting you, what do you think of? Armor that protects your whole body? A bubble that surrounds you so mean words or dangers bounce off you? Yeah, sometimes that kind of protection would be nice, wouldn't it?

But that's not always the way God works. Sometimes the protection He gives you comes from inside you. He makes you strong enough to stand up against temptation. He gives you peace when it seems like there is chaos all around you. He helps you be the person you've always been capable of being.

ChallengePoint

Wow, it's cool to think that God sometimes doesn't just put a bubble around you to protect you. Sometimes He works in your heart and helps you be a stronger person. That means He is helping you grow up to be an amazing man of God.

Seeking His Protection

I find true comfort, LORD, because Your laws have stood the test of time.

Psalm 119:52

How do you feel about rules? Following rules can be frustrating. The thing is, rules are put in place to protect you. Hopefully, they keep you from doing dumb things or making bad choices.

It helps to view rules like the walls of a house that keep you safe from dangers of all kinds. God's laws and regulations are rules to live by. While it may sometimes seem like His commands are hard to keep, they give you guidelines to know what is right and what is wrong. In the long run that makes life easier.

ChallengePoint

God gives laws and commands because He loves you. He wants you to be safe. He wants to help you learn to be a stronger Christian and a better person. When you think of God's laws like that, they are a comfort.

Serving Him

Two people are better than one, because they get more done by working together.

Ecclesiastes 4:9

Baseball is played on a team. There really is no way to play a game like baseball by yourself – no matter how good a player you are. Sometimes being part of a team is a good thing. God knew that. That's why this verse encourages teamwork and friendship. There is strength in numbers.

Friends and team-mates encourage you to be the best player you can be. They pick you up when you stumble. They cover for you when you're down. Now, here's some great news ... you're on God's team. He does all those things for you too.

ChallengePoint

Serving God can be lonely sometimes. But the realization that part of serving Him means you are on His team is an encouragement. Look around at the people God has placed in your life who can be your team-mates too. That's why God put them there!

"He must become greater; I must become less."

John 3:30

Are you a "behind-the-scenes" kind of guy? Do you enjoy being a supporter who helps the guys out front look good? Are you happy to get no attention or praise?

OK, put that thought on hold for a minute and think about this: Does it kind of seem like a no-brainer to say that serving God is important? OK, but are you willing to become more and more of a background person as you serve Him and He becomes more and more important? You'd better be, 'cause if you serve Him completely, that's what will happen. God must always be #1.

ChallengePoint

As God becomes #1, your desires and needs will kind of fade to the background. You'll be more and more eager to do what He wants and to serve Him in any way you can. And ... amazingly ... you'll be more filled with joy than ever!

Obeying Him

"No one can serve two masters. For you will hate one and love the other; you will be devoted to one and despise the other. You cannot serve both God and money."

Matthew 6:24

If you say you are a God-follower on Sunday, do you live like one on Tuesday, Friday or Saturday? You see, the thing about God is this ... either you're on His team or you're not.

If you try to ride the fence and be "on God's team" today, but do your own thing tomorrow, you will end up resenting God. If you're going to choose to obey God and serve Him ... do it. He won't accept half of your heart. God insists on full-service followers.

ChallengePoint

Some guys try to fake obeying God when what they really want is to do their own thing. They are trying to "serve two masters." They aren't fooling God though. Remember, He sees the heart so He knows where a person's loyalty is. Don't try to serve God and something else too. Give God your whole heart.

Be on your guard and stay awake. Your enemy, the devil, is like a roaring lion, sneaking around to find someone to attack.

1 Peter 5:8

The subject is video games. The topic is how the games work. In many of the games, you try to get from Point A to Point B, and so on, so you can move on to the next level. The problem is that there is some bad guy or some barrier that is always trying to trip you up and make you fail. It makes the game more challenging and fun.

But in real life, the devil tries to trip you up and keep you from obeying God. That's not fun. God warns you about the devil. He knows what a creep the devil is.

ChallengePoint

God warns you to stay alert and pay attention because He wants your obedience. He will help you fight off Satan's attacks. God never leaves you to fight alone. If obeying God is very important to you, ask Him for help. He will be there for you.

You are a gift to the world,
a divine work of art,
signed by God.
– Max Lucado

May

Knowing God by

His Forgiveness

May 1

"Come back to Me, you unfaithful children, and I will forgive you for being unfaithful." Yes, we will come to You, because You are the LORD our God.

Jeremiah 3:22

God wants to forgive you. That's pretty cool, isn't it? Since it's for sure that you will disobey Him by choosing to do your own thing, it's cool to know that He wants to forgive you.

However, forgiveness requires something from you. God asks you to choose to come back to Him; choose to ask His forgiveness. That's not hard when you recognize who God is and how much He loves you.

ChallengePoint

When such an amazing gift as forgiveness from almighty God is offered to you, it only makes sense to accept it. God doesn't require much from you. He just wants you to come to Him. That's not hard. It just means admitting your failures and asking Him for help.

Seeking Guidance

May 2

He gives me new strength. He leads me on paths that are right for the good of His name.

Psalm 23:3

Have you ever tried learning to do something new? You probably found that it is hard and takes a lot of work. You spend a lot of time practicing this new thing and give it a lot of energy. But one day you just feel as though you've given all you have to give and you just decide not to try anymore. So you slip back to doing things the way you used to do them and just forget about the new thing.

That's where one element of God's guidance comes in. He gently picks you up, gives you more energy and a little push on the shoulder to get you going down the right path.

ChallengePoint

God will guide your life. Yes, that sounds amazing – the God of creation cares about little old you. But He does and He will give you strength to keep growing and learning.

Surely your goodness and love will be with me all my life, and I will live in the house of the Lord forever.

Psalm 23:6

A guy who is a total baseball fan – absolutely LOVES the game – gets to go see his favorite team play. This fan gets to the game early and stands by the field watching warm-ups. His favorite player of all time is out on the field tossing the ball around. Oh wow, the fan would LOVE it if his hero noticed him standing there and took it upon himself to come over and chat.

Typically that wouldn't happen. Famous people don't go looking for their fans. They come when the fans shout and call to them. Then they sign an autograph and take off again to their busy lives. God – the most famous and important Person of all – is not like that. He pursues you. That means He's running after you, calling you to come to Him!

ChallengePoint

Why does God pursue you? 'Cause He loves you! He wants to fill your life with His goodness and His love. He wants to bless you. So stop running and look around you. God is there. Spend some time with Him!

Everyone has sinned; we all fall short of God's glorious standard.

Romans 3:23

Number One: God created people in His image. That means people were perfect.

Number Two: The first people sinned by disobeying God. That changed all people for the rest of time from perfect to broken – all people are sinners.

Number Three: God sent Jesus to earth to die for all the sins of people so that people can come to heaven.

Number Four: That means Jesus died for you.

Why did God come up with this plan? Simple ... 'cause He loves you.

ChallengePoint

You can convince yourself that you never do anything wrong ... that you're a pretty good guy. You may even be able to convince other people of that. But you'll never convince God, because He knows your thoughts and any secret things you do. Everyone sins. But because of God's amazing love for you, He came up with a plan to help you.

Continue praying, keeping alert, and always thanking God.

Colossians 4:2

Why does God say to pray all the time? Because talking with someone is how you get to know them. God wants to know what you're thinking about.

Why does He say to pray with an alert mind? A couple of reasons: Because the devil is always trying to mess up your life. And because when you are paying attention, you notice the things God is doing for you.

Why should you be thankful? When you do notice the ways God takes care of you and the things He does for you, it only follows that you will thank Him.

ChallengePoint

How good does it feel to be thanked when you do something for someone else? Really good, right? God does more for you than anyone else ever could. So why not thank Him?

Celebrating Him

May 6

Shout for joy to the LORD, all the earth, burst into jubilant song with music; make music to the LORD with the harp, with the harp and the sound of singing, with trumpets and the blast of the ram's horn – shout for joy before the LORD, the King.

Psalm 98:4-6

Sports fans go psycho with celebrating. What does that mean? When a fan supports a team, he cheers for them through the whole season. He's sad when they lose. He agonizes when they struggle. He stands by them no matter what, and would never cheer for their biggest competitors. When his team wins the championship he celebrates! You've seen it – a guy dancing around with arms waving in the air, cheering, screaming, whistling – whatever way he can show his joy.

Have you celebrated God that way? Why would you? Hey, if you take time to celebrate Him, you also take time to actually name the things to celebrate.

ChallengePoint

Naming things to celebrate means that you stop and take notice of all God has done in this world and all He does for you every day. There is so much to celebrate that you need to do a happy dance every day!

I focus on this one thing: Forgetting the past and looking forward to what lies ahead, I press on to reach the end of the race and receive the heavenly prize for which God, through Christ Jesus, is calling us.

Philippians 3:13-14

Quitters never win and winners never quit." "When the going gets tough, the tough get going." These famous quotes are about endurance. Life is going to be hard sometimes. There's not much you can do about it. Bad things happen. Things that are worthwhile take a lot of work. That's just the way it is.

When you have problems or when bad things happen, ask God for strength to get through it. Ask Him to help you keep on going. He will give you strength and help. He will help you keep on going.

ChallengePoint

If you quit trying when things get hard, you'll never grow stronger as a Christian and you will develop the habit of not finishing things you start. That's not good. God wants to help you learn and grow. He will give you endurance to get through the tough things. All you have to do is follow His guidance.

Training your body helps you in some ways, but serving God helps you in every way by bringing you blessings in this life and in the future life, too.

1 Timothy 4:8

Some people spend a lot of energy trying to get their bodies in shape. They run several miles every day or go to the gym for daily workouts. They slurp down energy drinks and carefully watch how much fat and sugar they put into their bodies. Taking care of their bodies almost become a full-time job.

It's a good idea to take care of your body, but don't forget your heart and soul. That means, don't forget the part of you that is constantly learning to know God better. Your heart obeys God and as it is "trained" you learn to love others the way God does. You learn to endure whatever life throws your way.

ChallengePoint

Training for godliness is kind of hard because it's such an up and down thing. It depends on your obedience and submission to God. But the benefits are amazing – not just a strong body like physical training, but a strong soul as you become more and more like God.

"The seeds that fell on good ground are the people who hear and understand the message. They produce as much as a hundred or sixty or thirty times what was planted."

Matthew 13:23

You may not have much experience at farming or even gardening, but here's a news flash: Flowers and vegetables need good soil to grow! Yep, they need healthy dirt. That's kind of a weird thing to say, but the bottom line is that good dirt has minerals and things in it that will help the seeds planted to grow into a plant and for the plant to grow its flower or vegetable.

Think about your heart in that way too. If God's Word is spoken to you or if you read it, then it lands in your heart. A healthy heart will let that seed settle in and begin to grow. When it grows your heart becomes more and more like Christ: kind, loving and obedient.

ChallengePoint

How do you get a healthy heart? It starts with giving your heart to Christ, and it stays healthy by talking with Him in prayer and asking Him to help you be obedient to Him. It's a series of choices every day to go God's way and not your own way.

Being Like Christ

Think about the things that are good and worthy of praise. Think about the things that are true and honorable and right and pure and beautiful and respected.

Philippians 4:8

If you put garbage in your mind, garbage is what will come out in your words and actions. That means if you watch junk on TV about violence, disrespect to others, programs filled with swearing ... those attitudes and even some of those actions will eventually start showing up in your life. That's because you get used to them and they don't seem so bad.

If you want your life to be like Christ's life, then fill your mind with things that are like Him. Read books or watch programs that have good messages. Spend time with people who model kindness and love. Put good stuff in, and good stuff will come out in the way you live.

ChallengePoint

Does that mean you can't watch TV or play video games? No, it just means be careful what kinds of messages you bombard your mind with. Choose things that are honoring to God and that will remind you to be like Christ.

Being Like Christ

When you are with unbelievers, always make good use of the time. Be pleasant and hold their interest when you speak the message. Choose your words carefully and be ready to give answers to anyone who asks questions.

Colossians 4:5-6

People are watching. All the time. Every word you say. Every thing you do. Every attitude you cop. All of these things show your own personal opinion of who God is. They show how important He truly is to you. Scary, huh?

It's true, though. That's why you are told to be smart about your actions and words, especially with those who don't know Christ. You can show others what Christ is like by living your life as He lived His. That's what God wants you to do. It's your foundational purpose for being in this world.

ChallengePoint

Foundational purpose? That's a grown-up phrase, isn't it? What does it mean? Just that your basic purpose for being here is to share God's love with others. One basic way you do that is by the way you live and the way you speak. Be careful. Make your words and actions count for Christ.

Knowing God by
Being Like Christ

Suppose someone has enough to live and sees a brother or sister in need, but does not help. Then God's love is not living in that person.

1 John 3:17

There are a lot of poor, hungry people in this world. Some live in your town. Some live in the nearest big city. Some live across the country. Some live in other countries. So what? So ... God says to help them.

Jesus said that the second most important command (second only to loving God) is to love others. If you love others, then when you see them hurting, you will want to help. Christ certainly did. When He saw people who needed something, whether it was food or healing, He took care of the problem.

ChallengePoint

OK, maybe you can't do miracles as Christ did. But you *can* do something. If you don't have a lot of money to give, you can volunteer at a soup kitchen or a homeless shelter. You can research what the needs are in your town, then make sure people know about those needs. Be like Christ by loving others.

Loving Others

Finally, all of you, live in harmony with one another; be sympathetic, love as brothers, be compassionate and humble.

1 Peter 3:8

OK, maybe this sounds weird. This Scripture verse tells you to agree with others and care about their feelings. Then it says to treat them like brothers and sisters. Yeah, how often do you get along with brothers and sisters that well? It's a known fact that brothers and sisters disagree and, yes, even argue and fight. HOWEVER, when push comes to shove and someone else starts picking on your brother or sister, you probably step up and defend them.

As you get older you'll probably get along with your brothers and sisters more. You will love them the way God says – with a tender and humble attitude.

ChallengePoint

God wants His children to get along. OK, sometimes that isn't easy, but it can be done with God's help. He is filled with love and He will share that love with you.

Showing Courage

If we endure hardship, we will reign with Him. If we deny Him, He will deny us.

2 Timothy 2:12

It's when the stuff of life gets tough that you find out how real your faith in God is. It is easy to claim you trust God when life is going smoothly. But when things like fights with your friends, parents splitting up, having to move to a new school or getting sick pop up – then you find out whether you really do trust God.

The thing is that you can claim to be a dynamite Christian and you can spout verses and prayers or whatever, which might convince other people that your faith in God is strong, but if it's really not, God will know. You can't fool Him. But He wants your faith to be real so that you courageously face whatever hard things happen.

ChallengePoint

If your faith in God is real then His strength will give you courage to handle life as it comes. Some hard things in life are painful. It's OK to hurt or to be sad, but God's strength will help you handle these hard things. Trust Him and depend on Him and your courage will grow!

It is by faith we understand that the whole world was made by God's command so what we see was made by something that cannot be seen.

Hebrews 11:3

Look up at the nighttime sky and you see a bazillion stars. Who made them?

Stand at the base of a mountain so high that its peaks are lost in the clouds. Who made it?

Look at the ocean so wide and deep that you can't imagine the actual size of it. Who made it?

Think of the giant redwood trees. A single tree is big enough to cut a hole through so a car can drive through it. Who made them?

Think about waterfalls so big and powerful that they power electricity for many cities. Who made them?

The flaming hot sun, the moon that controls the tides ... who made them? You know the answer to all of these questions ... God. Even more amazing is that everything in nature was made by Him ... from nothing!

ChallengePoint

God's power as revealed in nature is truly amazing. He made everything from scratch! And as His child, that power is available to help and guide you in life.

Trusting Him

May 16

The LORD has chosen you to be His own people. He will always take care of you so that everyone will know how great He is.

1 Samuel 12:22

Hopefully you know some people you trust; people who will stand up for you and be there for you no matter what. More than likely your family is in that category and hopefully some friends too. Have you thought about this though?

The main, Numero Uno person you can trust is ... God. He doesn't deal with the "what about me?" feelings that people sometimes have. God promises to stick with you, guide you, protect you and just plain old LOVE you. That will never change ... He promises.

ChallengePoint

People change. Sometimes their own feelings get in the way of promises to support you. God doesn't change. He does not break His promises. He never changes. You can always count on Him.

Knowing God by

His Love

May 17

The LORD is kind and shows mercy. He does not become angry quickly but is full of love.

Psalm 145:8

God expects the best from you. His constant, unfailing love for you means that He wants you to succeed. He wants the best for you. That means He is willing to forgive you when you fail. It means He is patient with you and that He doesn't have an explosive temper. He cares about you and will give you chance after chance to obey Him.

There is nothing else on earth to compare to God's love. It's deeper, stronger and more amazing than any human love.

ChallengePoint

Maybe you've heard about God's love all your life. Maybe you've heard about it so often that you don't really listen any more. Don't do that. Read this Scripture verse again and think about what it means to you. God loves you very much. That love shows in His patience, forgiveness and steadiness. He wants the best for you. Does His amazing love for you make you love Him more?

Praying

Listen to my voice in the morning, LORD. Each morning I bring my requests to You and wait expectantly.

Psalm 5:3

What are you like in the morning? When your mom or dad says its time to get up, do you pull the covers over your head and make them call you over and over? Then, when you finally drag yourself out of bed, are you grumpy for a while? In other words, do you wake up slowly?

The psalmist thought it was a good idea to start his day by talking to God. God must think that's a good idea too, since this Scripture verse is in the Bible. Why would He think that? Simple. Start your day by talking to God and thinking about Him and there is a better chance that your connection to Him will be strong all day. God wants to be part of your entire day.

ChallengePoint

God wants to be part of your entire day because He loves you. If you start your day by talking with Him, then He can guide you through the day. He will help you make good choices. He will listen as you explain the things that concern you, and then He will take care of them.

Seeking His Protection

The LORD defends those who suffer; He defends them in times of trouble.

Psalm 9:9

OK, so you are a big, tough guy who isn't afraid of anything, right? That means you don't need protection or a place to hide. Hiding is for scaredy cats, right? Yeah, right. It's not a crime to be afraid sometimes. In fact, it's kind of smart because some things in this world are downright scary.

The truth is that everyone is afraid of something, whether they admit it or not. People hide in different ways: by being mean and bossy and picking on weaker people, by acting tough, by losing themselves in a hobby or sports. However, the best place to go for protection when you're scared or in trouble is God. He's got power over everything, so He's the safest hiding place.

ChallengePoint

How do you "hide" in God? It's kind of a confusing concept, isn't it? You hide in God by studying His Word so you know what His promises to you are. You hide in Him by talking to Him every day and telling Him how you're feeling. You hide in Him by learning to trust Him to take care of you.

Serving Him

"What will you gain, if you own the whole world but destroy yourself?"

Mark 8:36

Movies, TV, music, the Internet, magazines, newspapers ... everything around you pounds into your head that success means a high-powered job earning lots of money. It means being famous or at the top of your career whether that is in business, entertainment or sports. OK, so maybe you are one of the few who do climb to the top? So what?

You may end up with all the money, power and fame in the world, but if you don't know God you have nothing. Know why? Because one day everyone dies. Everyone. Eternity is what's ahead and if you don't know God you spend forever in hell ... not fun.

ChallengePoint

Knowing God means that you've asked Jesus into your heart. When you've done that, you want to serve Him ... you just want to. The talents and abilities He gives you may take you to the top of your career. You may even become famous and earn lots of money – but that's not your ultimate goal. Serving God and pleasing Him is your goal.

Serving Him

In His grace, God has given us different gifts for doing certain things well. So if God has given you the ability to prophesy, speak out with as much faith as God has given you.

Romans 12:6

Do you know how it feels when a big group of guys line up to be chosen for teams ... and you are the last one picked? Yeah, it stinks, doesn't it? It's no fun to feel that you aren't very good at something.

Everyone wants to be recognized as being good – at least at one thing. You may not know what your "thing" is yet, but you *are* good at something. God gives each of His children some special gift. As your faith in Him grows strong and you learn to obey Him and follow Him, that "thing" will become evident. Once you know what your gift is, use it for Him.

ChallengePoint

Some people know their gift at a very young age. Others see it develop as they mature. Some gifts are obvious, like prophesying, preaching, or healing. Some are quieter gifts, like the ability to be a caring friend. Gifts from God are things you enjoy doing for Him and for others. When you know what your gift is, use it for God!

Serving Him

Do not let anyone treat you as if you are unimportant because you are young. Instead be an example to the believers with your words, your actions, your faith, and your pure life.

1 Timothy 4:12

Do you get tired of hearing ... "Someday when you're older, you can do this or that?" Yeah, that is frustrating. You could end up feeling as though life is on hold and what you're doing right now is just kids' stuff. Well, it's not true.

God doesn't waste a minute of your time. You can serve Him right now. The way you live – treating others with kindness and respect, being helpful, being humble, being honest – is an example to others of who God is.

ChallengePoint

Yeah, the way you live NOW shows others that you love God. When other kids your age see you living for God, that may have more impact on them than anything that a grown-up could say or do. You can serve God right now just by the way you live.

Obeying Him

How can a young person stay pure? By obeying Your word.

Psalm 119:9

No one likes rules. Don't think that once you're grown up you won't have to deal with rules because that just isn't true. Grown-ups have rules too – laws, rules at work and God's rules on how to live and how to treat others. There are some good things about rules. They give you guidelines to live by.

That's what God's Word does. If you know what He says in His Word then you know when you're disobeying Him. You will also know of His forgiveness and love. Everyone messes up sometimes. That doesn't make it okay, but God constantly forgives, loves and teaches you to do better the next time.

ChallengePoint

Thank goodness for God's forgiveness and love. Disobeying doesn't mean He turns His back on you. He will help you learn from your mistakes. He gave you the Bible to help you learn. It's His words of guidance and instruction. Read it and learn.

Obeying Him

Jesus said, "No, blessed are those who hear the teaching of God and obey it."

Luke 11:28

God does not insist that you obey His laws just because He wants to be the "Boss." The laws God put in place and wants you to obey will protect you and help you.

They will help you get along with other people, which will mean that you (and the people around you) enjoy life more. God's laws are for your own good. Is it hard to always obey? Yes. Is it worth it? Yes.

ChallengePoint

No, it isn't easy to always obey. But when you stop resisting obedience and realize that God's laws protect you from bad choices that could majorly mess up your life, and realize that they guide you in how to treat other people, well, obeying is a lot easier.

Obeying Him

Children, obey your parents in the Lord, for this is right.

Ephesians 6:1

God cares whether or not you obey your parents. Why? Because they are responsible to Him for teaching you and raising you to be a responsible adult. One of their responsibilities is to teach you about God and make you familiar with His Word. It is a big responsibility for them and it is more difficult when a child is rebellious.

Obeying your parents is really for your own good. There may be times when it doesn't seem like it, but if you think about the big picture of your whole life, you will see that obeying them teaches you a lot.

ChallengePoint

Obeying your parents honors God. It follows the path He put in place, which leads to obeying Him. Everyone has trouble obeying sometimes, but make every effort to learn from your mistakes and obey more each day. It honors God and it honors your parents.

Obeying Him

Don't you know that you are slaves of anyone you obey? You can be slaves of sin and die, or you can be obedient slaves of God and be acceptable to Him.

Romans 6:16

Stubbornly rebelling against God by refusing to obey His laws does not mean you are free. Sorry if you thought it did. The truth is that you belong to something or someone. If you choose to run with a rough crowd of guys and do the things they do, then you become a slave to that kind of life and your heart belongs to sin.

Complete freedom doesn't exist – you belong to something. God encourages you to belong to Him because that leads to eternal life in heaven. It's a good thing.

ChallengePoint

God encourages obedience to Him because in the big picture of life it is the best thing for you … on this earth and in the life to come. He knows that you will get sucked into something – it's the human way. Focus your heart on Him and make every effort to obey Him.

Seeking His Guidance

Lord, since I have many enemies, show me the right thing to do. Show me clearly how You want me to live.

Psalm 5:8

Have you ever played the game where you are blind-folded and instructed to walk around a room by another person? They can only speak to you, not touch you or lead you by the hand. You have to trust that your guide won't walk you into something that will hurt you or put you in a position of danger.

That's not something you have to worry about when God guides your entire life. He wants to guide you. Sometimes it may seem like He is hiding His instructions and you can't figure out what He wants from you. But more than likely, you're not putting yourself in a place to recognize His guidance.

ChallengePoint

God wants to guide your life. He gave you the Bible. He also will speak to your heart if you ask for His guidance, become quiet and listen to what He says. There may be times in your life when it seems as though God isn't speaking – in those times, keep on doing what you're doing. That's probably exactly what He wants. If it isn't, He will let you know.

His Faithfulness

Give your burdens to the LORD, and He will take care of you.
He will not permit the godly to slip and fall.

Psalm 55:22

What's the heaviest load you've ever carried? Maybe it was a backpack full of books. Whatever it was, it probably got heavier and heavier the longer you walked. When you put it down, did your arm and back muscles shout, "THANK YOU!"?

Some of the things you carry around in your heart get pretty heavy too, don't they? Grief, guilt, worry and other emotions weigh you down. Guess what? You can get rid of them. God wants to take them off your back and help you. You can always count on Him too, because He is faithful – He will always do what He says He will do.

ChallengePoint

OK, so exactly how do you give things to God? It's not always easy to stop your worrying or grieving. You have to continually ask God to take the worry or grief away. Ask Him to take care of the situations, and when the worry or grief pops back into your mind, just remind yourself that God is taking care of it and that you can trust Him to do so.

Seeking Salvation

May 29

I mean that you have been saved by grace through believing.
You did not save yourselves; it was a gift from God. It was
not the result of your own efforts, so you cannot brag
about it.

Ephesians 2:8-9

You can't buy it. You can't earn it. You can't bargain for it, study for it or beg for it. Salvation is a gift. God gives you the chance to accept His gift of salvation from your sin and the future of forever being separated from Him just because He loves you. Yep, He loves you and really wants you to be a part of His family.

Grace is the reason – grace means that He gives this gift even though you don't deserve it (no one does) and you've done nothing to earn it. He forgives your sins, loves you, and saves you because of His grace.

ChallengePoint

Have you accepted God's gift of salvation? That means praying a prayer admitting your sin, confessing it, and asking forgiveness as you ask Jesus to come into your heart and be your Savior. It's a gift because of God's amazing love for you.

Enduring

When you have many kinds of troubles, you should be full of joy.

James 1:2

R-i-i-i-g-g-h-h-t-t ... yahoo for problems! Is that what this Scripture verse means? Kind of ... not exactly. Why should you consider trouble something to celebrate? Because of what you can learn from it:

1. You learn to trust God because He will get you through it.
2. You learn that there is strength inside you that you never knew you had.
3. Your faith will grow stronger as you see that God is always willing to help you.

ChallengePoint

Endurance is when you keep on plodding through problems and difficulties. That's a whole lot easier to do when you know God is working on things for you. When you have problems, go to Him right away and see what happens and what you can learn!

A gentle answer deflects anger, but harsh words make tempers flare.

Proverbs 15:1

You've heard the expression WWJD ... What Would Jesus Do? But have you thought about WWJS ... What Would Jesus Say? Don't think that means you have to be a meek, quiet thing. Jesus wasn't a wimp when He walked on this earth.

When someone was messing up and needed to be told, Jesus told them ... but His words were always couched with love and concern for those around Him.

If one man was teaching or doing something that was going to hurt someone else, Jesus set him straight. When someone attacked Him, He didn't respond with angry words; His responses were straightforward but gentle. There's a lesson there.

ChallengePoint

When someone gets angry with you and shouts angry words, how do you respond? If you get angry and shout back, then the situation is going to get worse. You can slow things down with a gentle response. That doesn't mean you have to take abuse, it means you don't respond with abuse. Gentleness is better.

Dare to be remarkable!
– Anonymous

June

"Do not judge, or you too will be judged."

Matthew 7:1

How do you feel when someone decides that you're not smart, you're unkind, you're not athletic, you're dishonest ... whatever. Being judged by people who don't really know you is no fun. It's not fair, either.

Jesus taught that judging others leads to being judged yourself – by God. He gave people a chance to prove themselves. Remember? He talked to hated tax collectors and women – people that the important people of society ignored.

Some of those tax collectors and women became powerful leaders of the church.

ChallengePoint

When you judge someone as not being "good" enough to be your friend, you might miss getting to know someone amazing. And you might miss the chance to encourage a person who could do amazing things for Christ!

Being Like Christ

Whatever you do or say, do it as a representative of the Lord Jesus, giving thanks through Him to God the Father.

Colossians 3:17

Think about what a representative does:

- He gives an impression of the company, team or person he represents to those who haven't had personal contact.
- He speaks to the public for the company, team or person he represents.
- He answers questions.
- He encourages others to become a supporter of what he represents.

That's what you do every day for God. The things you say and the things you do give others an impression of who God is.

ChallengePoint

Jesus was God's representative by speaking and acting with love for God and love for others. That was His constant focus. Is your love for God and others always the first thing people will see?

Being Like Christ

In your lives you must think and act like Christ Jesus. Christ Himself was like God in everything. But He did not think that being equal with God was something to be used for His own benefit. But He gave up His place with God and made Himself nothing. He was born as a man and became like a servant.

Philippians 2:5-7

If there was ever anyone who had reason to think He deserved good treatment, it was Jesus. After all, He was a human, but He was also God.

As you read about His life on earth though, you'll never read about Him being full of pride or arrogance. He treated others with respect. He even served others – washing the feet of His disciples is a good example of that. Pride had no place in His heart. Jesus cared for others.

ChallengePoint

Do you care more about yourself or others? Who is first in your heart? If it's others, you will be willing to serve them. That means doing things that you'd rather not do sometimes or doing things for others rather than yourself. It isn't always easy, but it is the way Jesus lived. A servant attitude is the model He gave you.

Being Like Christ

Let us think of ways to motivate one another to acts of love and good works.

Hebrews 10:24

Jesus is all about bringing out the best in people. When He was on earth He encouraged people to know God better, which meant that they should treat others with love and look for ways to serve others.

Do you give that kind of encouragement to others too? It means that you have to stop thinking only of yourself. You must be willing to sometimes be in the background cheering someone else on.

ChallengePoint

Are you willing to be a background person who encourages someone else to be the "star" once in a while? It's not easy. But being like Christ means that you don't think only of yourself. You look for ways to encourage and motivate others to be the kind of people God wants them to be. To do that, you have to be behind the scenes.

"The greatest way to show love for friends is to die for them."

John 15:13

Duhh, I don't get it. How is it gonna help my friend if I get hit by a truck or something?" OK, dude. That's not what this Scripture verse means.

Lay down your life in this Scripture verse can mean several things. Certainly Jesus laid down His life by dying, but He also laid it down by *giving*. He served others so He gave up His own plans, agenda, and desires. He laid those things down. Get it?

ChallengePoint

Lay down your life for others by focusing on what's best for them. Give up your ideas of how to spend your time and energy. Serve others by helping and encouraging them. Share God's love with others by giving, giving and giving some more. Time, energy, encouragement, money ... whatever they need.

This is how God showed His love to us: He sent His one and only Son into the world so that we could have life through Him. This is what real love is: It is not our love for God; it is God's love for us. He sent His Son to die in our place to take away our sins.

1 John 4:9-10

What's your most prized possession? The thing that you don't want anyone else to touch without your permission? The thing that you hide from your little brother or sister? Would you willingly give that thing away? Yeah, that would be tough. God did though.

God gave Someone He loved very much to a bunch of people who ignored the gift and even tortured then killed the gift ... which, of course, was Jesus. God gave His Son willingly, knowing that Jesus would be tortured, abused and killed by the very people He was given to. Why? Why would He give so generously? Simple ... love. God loves people. God loves you.

ChallengePoint

God's love is a gift to you. All you need to do is receive it. Thank Him for it. His gift of Jesus is just one proof of His love. Every day, in a multitude of ways, He says that He loves you. Listen ... and tell Him you love Him too.

Be strong and courageous! Do not be afraid or discouraged.
For the LORD your God is with you wherever you go.

Joshua 1:9

Being thrown into a battle without the right equipment would be scary ... not to mention dangerous. A soldier would have his helmet, his weapon and whatever else he needed to be as safe as possible.

Being as prepared as possible for battle would give you a bit more courage, right? Well, dude, you've got the one thing you need to be the bravest, most courageous guy ever. God. Yep. He promised to be with you, help you, strengthen you, go before you, bring up the rear behind you – in other words, protect you completely.

ChallengePoint

If God is with you and all around you, what is there to be afraid of? OK, let's be realistic. You will be afraid sometimes and you know what? – that's OK. But when you feel the fear start rolling around inside you, remind yourself that God is with you. Focus on that thought and let it cover over the fear. It may take a while, but it will overcome your fear.

He gives strength to those who are tired and more power to those who are weak.

Isaiah 40:29

You know, it's one thing to read about God's power. And it is interesting to read about how He helped Joshua or Moses in the Bible. It's also encouraging to hear how He strengthened someone in the world today. But what means the most is experiencing His power *yourself*. How does that happen? OK, here's a suggestion:

1. When you have a problem, ask God to help you.
2. Look up verses about His power and strength.
3. Memorize one that you really like.
4. Say it over and over – especially when you're afraid or just worn out from fear.
5. Notice the little things that happen; an encouraging word from a friend, something that is usually difficult gets easier. See the small ways God helps you.
6. Eventually you will see that God's strength and power is growing in you!

ChallengePoint

Try this list of six steps to see if you can experience more of God's strength and power in your life.

Giving

June 9

If we have all we need and see one of our own people in need, we must have pity on that person, or else we cannot say we love God.

1 John 3:17

The news reports are often filled with images of people around the world who do not have enough ... of anything. They don't have to wonder what to choose for dinner at night – they wonder if they will have any dinner. They don't have to choose what to wear each day – the clothes on their backs are all they have. Some have no homes, no jobs and they don't even have the stuff you consider basic to life.

God did not place you on this earth so that you could get as much stuff as possible and wrap your arms around it while shouting, "MINE!" like a two-year-old. Those who know God will help others by giving what they have ... it shows that God's love is important to them.

ChallengePoint

It's basically impossible to really, truly love God but ignore the needs of people around the world. People who are suffering because of war, drought, floods or earthquakes need your help. In whatever way you can help them. It's the "God-thing" to do.

Knowing God by

Suppressing Our Pride

Always be humble and gentle. Be patient with each other, making allowance for each other's faults because of your love.

Ephesians 4:2

Four guidelines:

1. Be humble – remember life isn't all about you. It's about God.
2. Be gentle – don't push other people around to get them to do what you want.
3. Be patient – things won't always go your way.
4. Make allowances for others' faults – everyone messes up sometimes – even you. Cut your friends and family some slack, just as you want them to do for you.

Why do all of this? Love. Yep. God's love flowing through you to others.

ChallengePoint

Doing these four things is a way to show God's love to others. If you can be humble, gentle, patient and make allowances it shows that you understand life isn't all about you. God said to love others and get over yourself. So … go for it.

Abiding in Him

"Remain in Me, and I will remain in you. A branch cannot produce fruit alone but must remain in the vine. In the same way, you cannot produce fruit alone but must remain in Me. I am the vine, and you are the branches. If any remain in Me and I remain in them, they produce much fruit. But without Me they can do nothing."

John 15:4-5

It doesn't take a rocket scientist to figure out that a branch chopped off a tree is going to die. The leaves will die. Any fruit or flowers will die.

God warns you about this same kind of starving-to-death experience. If you don't stay connected to Him, your soul will literally starve to death. You need to be fed from His Word, by His love, and with His Spirit in you. If you don't stay connected to Him, then the things He planned for you to do in life will not happen. What a waste.

ChallengePoint

You have an opportunity to make your life count for something. But that will only happen if you stay connected to God. Get your spiritual food from Him. Let Him guide and direct you. Do what He has planned for you.

Knowing God by
Trusting Him

Let us hold firmly to the hope that we have confessed, because we can trust God to do what He promised.

Hebrews 10:23

When you say you're going to do something, do people know that they can count on you to do it? Can you be totally trusted to follow through? If so, that's great. Not all people can be counted on.

God wants you to know that you can absolutely, without a doubt every single time, count on Him. When God says He will do something – it's law!

ChallengePoint

When you read that God will do what He says, does the question cross your mind … what does He say? There's only one way to find out – read the Bible. It is God's words to you. When you read something God promises in it, then count on it. You can depend on Him and lean on Him. He's more solid than rock.

Using His Gifts

Christ chose some of us to be apostles, prophets, missionaries, pastors, and teachers, so that His people would learn to serve and His body would grow strong.

Ephesians 4:11-12

A baseball team has a catcher, pitcher, first baseman, shortstop ... a player for every position. In order for the team to win, each player must do his job – play his position.

God put you on His "team" and gave you a special job to do. You have special abilities and talents that God gave you in order to help His work be done. Maybe you don't yet know what those abilities are, but as you keep learning about God, He will show you.

ChallengePoint

Do you sometimes feel like "I'm just a kid, I can't do anything for God"? Well, that's not true. Read through the Bible and you'll read of some kids doing amazing things. Ask God to show you how He wants to use you. Think about what kinds of things you enjoy doing and that people often say you're good at. Your gifts probably are in that area.

Knowing God by

His Love

The LORD your God is with you; the mighty One will save you.
He will rejoice over you. You will rest in His love; He will sing
and be joyful about you.

Zephaniah 3:17

Perhaps you've heard all your life that God loves you.
So by now it's "old news" that you just kind of brush
aside. If that's the case, stop right now and really think
about this – the God of the universe, God who created
everything there is, God who controls the oceans, the
weather, makes the stars stay in the sky ... that God loves
YOU.

He not only loves you, He lives right here with you ...
among His people. You make Him happy; so happy that
He sings songs about you.

ChallengePoint

The truth that you make God happy – so happy that He
sings songs about you – should take away any thoughts
of "Yeah, yeah, I've heard that before!" Does it make you
feel really special? It should. God loves you ... YOU!

Knowing God by

Praying

June 15

Pray without ceasing.

1 Thessalonians 5:17

Pray all the time? Every minute of the day? Seriously? What about eating, sleeping, talking to my friends, doing homework, playing sports?"

If that's your reaction to this verse, you have something to learn about yourself. It is possible to do more than one thing at a time. Seriously. All the time you're doing those other things, thoughts are running through the back of your mind.

If your desire is to be in constant prayer, then you can focus those background thoughts as prayers. So, say you're walking down the street and you see an elderly person working in his yard. Your background prayer might be, "God, thank You that this man can be outside today. Give Him strength to do His work."

ChallengePoint

Praying all the time means that your thoughts constantly go back to God and you're aware of people around you and pray for them – just a short prayer of one sentence, but still a prayer.

Seeking His Protection

I waited patiently for the LORD. He turned to me and heard my cry.

Psalm 40:1

The interesting thing about this Scripture verse is the word "patiently." When you are afraid because you're in danger and waiting to be rescued, it is only possible to wait patiently if you absolutely trust that someone is coming to help you.

That means when you cry out to God for help and do not immediately sense His action, you don't give up. You KNOW He will help. He promised to hear your prayer and you know that He loves you and will take care of you. Seeking His protection only happens with trust.

ChallengePoint

The trust that waits patiently for God's help comes in stages. Don't be discouraged if you don't feel you have that kind of trust right now. Trust in seeking His protection grows when you see a small way in which He protects you. Then the next time you seek His protection your trust is a little stronger.

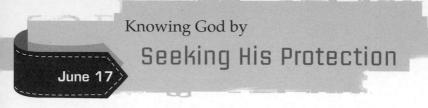

Seeking His Protection

June 17

He heals the brokenhearted and binds up their wounds.

Psalm 147:3

Here's the struggle: God can do anything. He has power over the whole world and anything that happens in it. So when your loved one gets really sick, why doesn't God just heal that person? You probably pray that He will do that. But He doesn't and your loved one dies. Is it hard then for you to find God in that situation?

God doesn't often change the natural course of events in this world. Bad things happen. People die. It stinks, but it's true. So where is God? Right there with you – loving you, caring for you, bandaging the wounds of your heart.

ChallengePoint

Of course you would prefer that God just fix the bad things – stop them from happening. But He doesn't always do that. However, when you hurt, He hurts, be-cause He loves you. His protection of you is to protect your heart when it's hurting because that's when it is most vulnerable to Satan. He bandages your heart by His love ... and protects you.

Serving Him

Jesus called out to them, "Come, follow Me, and I will show you how to fish for people."

Mark 1:17

Um, fish ... for people?" That's weird, huh? Okay, Jesus didn't mean that you would actually pull people out of a lake with your fishing rod. That's just silly.

When He said this He was talking to fishermen, and Jesus often used examples that made sense to the people He was talking to. The point of Jesus' comment is that He will show you how to influence people to want to know Him.

ChallengePoint

Not every person is a great preacher. Not everyone is good at sharing their faith with people on the street. But every Christian has abilities to be used in God's service that will be a part of others coming to know Christ. Cool, huh?

We don't have the right to claim that we have done anything on our own. God gives us what it takes to do all that we do.
2 Corinthians 3:5

No one enjoys being around a bragger. Someone who's always spouting, "Yeah me! I'm so cool! I'm the best!" kind of stuff doesn't really know the score. He had nothing to do with the very things he's bragging about.

All abilities come from God. Oh, it's true that you can work to develop and strengthen your abilities – things like athletic abilities or musical talent – but the basic talent, and even the strength and drive to develop it, comes from God. No person has any reason to brag about anything.

ChallengePoint

God made you able to do what you can do. But He didn't just give you those skills to make the world a better place. He wants you to use them for Him. That may mean something as simple (and easy) as giving Him the credit for your successes instead of holding a "Hurray for me" party.

Serving Him

Be careful to live properly among your unbelieving neighbors. Then even if they accuse you of doing wrong, they will see your honorable behavior, and they will give honor to God when He judges the world.

1 Peter 2:12

You go to church and Sunday school. You attend the midweek club program at your church. You pray before meals and before drifting off to sleep at night. Maybe you even read your Bible during the week. So ... you're good, right? Well, kind of. There's a lot more to serving God.

How do you treat the people around you? Do you throw a temper tantrum when your team loses – especially getting angry at the team-mate you feel lost the game? How do you react to a friend when he wins at a board game you're playing? How honest are you in keeping score? What kinds of things do you say about other people? The point is that how you live means something, especially to people who do not know Christ.

ChallengePoint

Have you thought about the fact that you are serving God by the everyday things you do? Scary, huh? People are watching you because you claim to be a Christian. Do they see God's love in you? They are watching.

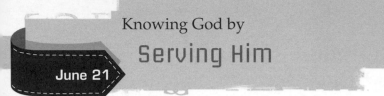

Knowing God by

Serving Him

June 21

Do your work willingly, as though you were serving the Lord Himself, and not just your earthly master.

Colossians 3:23

No doubt there are some things that you do just because you have to do them. Your enthusiasm is not so great for those jobs. That may mean that you don't do your best work, but just do enough to get by.

That won't cut it when you're doing God's work. When you are serving God, do your best – no matter what the job is. It may seem that what you're doing is a behind the scenes, not important, job. But anything done for God deserves your best.

ChallengePoint

So … how do you know when the work you're doing is God's work? The thing is that every job you do is God's work because other people are watching you. How you do your job reflects your opinion of God. So … always do your best and remember that you're doing this job for God, not for people.

Obeying Him

LORD, tell me Your ways. Show me how to live.

Psalm 25:4

Imagine two roads in front of you. Which road you go down is your choice. If someone comes up to you and says, "Take the one on the right," would you take it? Or would you take the one on the left just because the other one was suggested?

If you're going to obey God, you need to be willing to follow what He tells you to do. God will show you the right path to take ... will you then be willing to take it?

ChallengePoint

A big part of obeying God is knowing what He wants you to do. The best way to learn that is by reading His Word and being still before Him so He can speak into your heart. He also guides through the advice and opinions of Christian people around you. Listen for His guidance, then be willing to follow it.

We can be sure that we know God if we obey His commands. Anyone who says, "I know God," but does not obey God's commands is a liar, and the truth is not in that person.

1 John 2:3-4

Blah, Blah, Blah!" You can say whatever you want about knowing God. But if your actions don't match what you say, then your words are just "Blah, Blah, Blah!"

Don't bother talking about knowing God if you are going to do things that are directly disobedient to Him. God says that makes you a liar.

ChallengePoint

You can't fool God. You can claim whatever you want to other people and maybe even convince them that you're obedient to God. But you can't fool Him. He insists on obedience … complete obedience.

His Forgiveness

The payment for sin is death. But God gives us the free gift of life forever in Christ Jesus our Lord.

Romans 6:23

You work at a job and you get paid. That's the way the system works. Does it surprise you that there is also payment for sin? Sounds kind of strange, doesn't it, that you should expect payment for doing wrong things? Well, the payment isn't good – it's being forever apart from God – death means being in hell forever.

But God's love makes forgiveness possible. He forgives your sin and changes the payment to life forever with Him!

ChallengePoint

God's forgiveness of your sin is motivated completely by His amazing love for you. He wants you to be in heaven with Him forever, so He takes away the payment of death and celebrates that you'll be with Him in heaven. Ask Him to forgive your sins … and thank Him when He does.

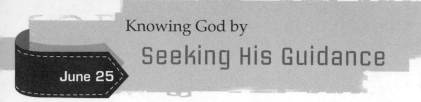

Seeking His Guidance

For the LORD grants wisdom! From His mouth comes knowledge and understanding.

Proverbs 2:6

Sometimes when a driver is stopped by a policeman for driving over the speed limit, he will say, "Oh, I didn't know what the speed limit was." Too bad – he'll probably get a ticket anyway because it is his responsibility to know the law.

In the same way, you shouldn't try telling God that you didn't know the right thing to do when you do something wrong. If you ever have a question about whether something is a good thing to do … ask Him. He's willing to guide you, and His guidance will be filled with wisdom.

ChallengePoint

God's guidance may not be as simple as, "Do this. Don't do that." Then again, it might be. After asking for His guidance, get into His Word and, as you read it, let your mind and heart kind of be quiet. You may find that a particular phrase or verse seems to jump off the page at you as God uses it to guide you. Then you will know – Do this. Don't do that.

Understanding Anger

Don't be angry or furious. Anger can lead to sin.

Psalm 37:8

Let's look at this situation:

1. Your friend makes you super-mad by saying some-thing mean or untrue about you. Or maybe he brags about beating you at a game. Whatever – you are super-ticked.
2. You're so mad that you completely lose control – you start shouting things at him without really thinking about what you're saying. All kinds of junk comes out of your mouth.
3. That friendship is toast – no chance of it being fixed.

God warns you against that kind of response. When you get that angry, relationships are damaged beyond control.

ChallengePoint

God's focus is you – how you respond and treat others. He also doesn't want your friendships or family relation-ships to be damaged beyond fixing. One way to prevent that is to keep your anger under control.

Being Faithful

LORD, the heavens praise You for Your miracles and for Your loyalty in the meeting of Your holy ones.

Psalm 89:5

One definition of faithfulness is conscientious. That means paying attention to detail from a sense of responsibility or devotion.

God surely shows faithfulness in His work with His children. He takes care of you. He loves you. He guides you. He teaches you. He planned a way of salvation for you. He planned heaven for you. No wonder heaven itself praises Him. No wonder the angels sing praises to Him.

ChallengePoint

God will never go against His own character. He is faithful. That's the bottom line. You can always depend on Him to do those things He promised to do for you. He's faithful. Praise Him for that.

His Faithfulness

If we are unfaithful, He remains faithful, for He cannot deny who He is.

2 Timothy 2:13

God has made some very strong promises to His children. He promises to love you, protect you, guide you ... and on and on.

What does He ask from you? To love Him. What happens if you don't act loving toward Him? What if you are disobedient and rebellious? Does He turn away from His promises? Nope. He can't because God is love. God is faithful. That's who He is and He simply cannot act any other way.

ChallengePoint

People's actions and moods change all the time. One day you're kind and helpful, and the next day you're a pain in the neck. With some people you don't know what you're going to get from day to day. God isn't like that. He is always the same. You can count on that. You can trust Him completely because you can know He will always be the loving God He promises to be.

Knowing God by

Seeking Salvation

If you confess with your mouth, "Jesus is Lord," and believe in your heart that God raised Him from the dead, you will be saved.

Romans 10:9

1. Confess with your mouth that Jesus is Lord. That means say it out loud ... publicly.
2. Believe that God raised Jesus from the dead. Believe it, don't just say it. Know for sure that it's true.
3. Salvation is yours. Jesus is now living in your heart – loving, guiding and teaching. Heaven is in your future – forever with God!

ChallengePoint

Becoming saved is not hard. God made the plan, but you have to open your heart to Him. It's not hard, but you do have to make the effort.

Being Thankful

No matter what happens, always be thankful, for this is God's will for you who belong to Christ Jesus.

1 Thessalonians 5:18

You get an unexpectedly good grade on a test – woohoo! You're thankful! Your team wins a championship – you shout thankfulness! A sick friend gets well, your mom or dad gets a great job, you're chosen for an honor ... when good things happen it's pretty easy to be thankful (if you remember to say thanks).

But when things happen that aren't exactly what you would have chosen for your life, are you thankful then? Yeah, that's harder. But God says to be thankful no matter what.

ChallengePoint

God is in control of everything. He has a plan for your life. If you believe those two things, then thankfulness should come more easily. OK, sometimes it's hard to be immediately thankful when difficult things happen, but if you believe those two statements, you will eventually be able to get to the thankful place.

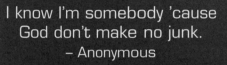

I know I'm somebody 'cause
God don't make no junk.
– Anonymous

July

The LORD your God has blessed everything you have done;
He has protected you while you traveled through this great
desert. The LORD your God has been with you for the past
forty years, and you have had everything you needed.

Deuteronomy 2:7

Celebrate God! Why? Because you can read this book. Because you have a home. Because you have a family who loves you. Because you can attend church, read the Bible, pray to Him. Because you go to school, go on vacation, go shopping and God watches every step.

He takes care of your every need (not "wants" but "needs"). Celebrate Him for all He does for you.

ChallengePoint

You know how great it feels to be thanked when you do something nice. It's even cooler for the thanks to be so grand that it's a celebration. God does so much for you every day – thank Him with grand, heartfelt celebrations!

Enduring

God is the one who began this good work in you, and I am certain that He won't stop before it is complete on the day that Christ Jesus returns.

Philippians 1:6

Endurance is often talked about as something you need to do – hanging in there when life gets tough. Did you know that God also has the characteristic of endurance? It's true. He started doing good stuff in your heart before you were even born or had accepted Jesus as your Savior.

He will keep that good work going all the way until Jesus comes again and you're in heaven with Him. He keeps teaching you and growing your faith so that you are more and more like Christ.

ChallengePoint

So what this verse is saying is that you are always "under construction." God is continually working on you. That's kind of cool when you think about it. He never stops working to help you be better – more mature in your faith and more like the person He wants you to be.

Being Like Christ

"I was hungry, and you gave Me food. I was thirsty, and you gave Me something to drink. I was alone and away from home, and you invited Me into your house. I was without clothes, and you gave Me something to wear. I was sick, and you cared for Me. I was in prison, and you visited Me."

Matthew 25:35-36

Think about others' needs before your own. That's a basic characteristic of being like Christ. Too many people spend too much time thinking about their own wants (not just needs) and how anything that happens affects them. People do not want to be inconvenienced by situations – even if that situation is tragic for someone else.

Jesus modeled caring for others first, without even thinking about how tired He was or what another day of healing people or teaching people meant to His tired body. He didn't worry about where His next meal was coming from or where He would sleep at night. He cared for others first and foremost.

ChallengePoint

These two verses show that being like Christ means caring for other people, and that by doing that you show your care for Christ Himself. Ask God to open your eyes to the needs of people around you.

For we are God's masterpiece. He has created us anew in Christ Jesus, so we can do the good things He planned for us long ago.

Ephesians 2:10

A masterpiece is an artist's finest creation. An artist puts his heart and soul into his artwork. Most artists have a certain style, so when you look at their artwork, you know that it was done by that particular artist.

That's true of God's masterpiece too. You are His masterpiece. He made you in His own image. That means you look like Him. And when you ask Jesus into your heart, you have even more of His fingerprints on you, so it's even more obvious who the Artist is!

ChallengePoint

Isn't it cool to know that being like Christ doesn't totally rest on your shoulders? You are God's masterpiece and you look like one of His creations. He has given you what you need to be more and more like Christ.

Solid food is for those who are grown up. They are mature enough to know the difference between good and evil.

Hebrews 5:14

You're hungry ... really hungry. So you go into the kitchen expecting Mom to make you a big sandwich and maybe some cut-up fruit or something to go with it. But she doesn't. Instead, she pulls out a baby bottle, filled to the brim with formula and hands that to you. Yuck ... not what you wanted, huh? You don't drink baby formula anymore; you've grown beyond that.

Becoming more and more like Christ in your Christian life is kind of like growing beyond baby formula. As you learn more about Him and become more like Him in the way you think and act, you can handle more Christian lessons and more responsibility.

ChallengePoint

Are you still drinking baby formula in your Christian life? Or are you learning more and more about Christ and becoming more like Him in how you live? If so, you are learning the difference between right and wrong – and choosing right is becoming a little easier every day.

Loving Others

"I am giving you a new command. You must love each other, just as I have loved you."

John 13:34

News flash: Life isn't all about you. The most important thing is NOT how you feel or what you think. You're supposed to be thinking about other people. Yep, God said it: Love each other.

He doesn't mean mushy, gushy love, but putting other people's needs before your own. It's caring about how they feel and what they are going through. Loving others the way God loves you is ... complete. Put yourself in the background and care for others.

ChallengePoint

Is this kind of love easy? Nope. Is it necessary even for people you don't like so much? Yep. Yikes! But you don't have to try to do it alone. You can ask God to love others through you – especially people who are kind of hard to love. He will do it ... and it takes a while, but pretty soon you'll start to notice a change in how you feel about those difficult people.

Loving Others

Love never gives up, never loses faith, is always hopeful, and endures through every circumstance.

1 Corinthians 13:7

Here's your model: God loves you, no matter what. You may break His commandments but He sticks with you time and time again. That's what love does.

Do you love Him back? No matter what? Do you trust Him completely, even when it feels as though He's not hearing your prayers and not doing what you think He should be doing? Do you love Him enough to trust Him, no matter what happens?

ChallengePoint

God's love is steady, strong, and hopeful. Because of that He always hopes you will be more obedient and grow to be more like Christ. Does your love for Him reflect that same kind of strength and persistence? Love Him, no matter what.

Showing Love

So we know the love that God has for us, and we trust that love. God is love. Those who live in love live in God, and God lives in them.

1 John 4:16

Famous people are often defined by the thing that made them famous. A famous professional baseball player is known for his baseball playing skill. A musician is known for his musical ability. A scientist for his research skills.

God is known by love. His character – the thing that defines God – is love. His love is seen throughout the Bible in the way He took care of His people. You can see it in your life in the way He cares for you and guides you.

ChallengePoint

God is love. That's it. That's the bottom line. You are His child, a member of His family. You should look like Him. Is His love evident in you?

Knowing God by

Showing Courage

July 9

Wait for the L<small>ORD</small>; be strong and take heart and wait for the L<small>ORD</small>.

Psalm 27:14

What does this verse have to do with knowing God better? Think about it ... when you're scared, you have a tendency to run around like a chicken with its head cut off trying to fix things or trying to find someone to help you.

But God says not to do that. He says to be brave enough not to run around like crazy. Instead, wait for Him to take care of things. You can trust Him because He loves you. So wait patiently and with courage for God to act.

ChallengePoint

Waiting is never easy. It's especially hard when you are afraid. But that is also the best time to learn that your faith in God can be trusted. He will take care of you. Be brave and be patient.

Finally, be strong in the Lord and in His great power.

Ephesians 6:10

The bottom line is this: Whatever happens, keep depending on God. Don't let anything pull you away from Him. You can trust Him because His power is mightier than anything else in this world.

What do you consider to be the most powerful thing in this world? Think about that for a minute. OK, now understand that God is more powerful than that. Way more powerful. So whatever you are facing, whatever is making you afraid, remember that you can trust God.

ChallengePoint

If you say that you trust God, then show it. When something happens that scares you – your parents splitting up; someone you love getting really sick; a tornado ripping through your town – whatever it is, you can trust God, because His power is stronger than any of those things. Fear not.

Knowing God by

Witnessing His Power

You made all the delicate, inner parts of my body and knit me together in my mother's womb. Thank You for making me so wonderfully complex! Your workmanship is marvelous – how well I know it. You watched me as I was being formed in utter seclusion, as I was woven together in the dark of the womb.

Psalm 139:13-15

A newborn baby has everything in his body that he needs to be an adult: the muscles he will need as a full-grown man are already there. The tiny, flexible bones in his feet will grow to be size 13 some day. His brain will develop to solve intricate math problems.

What's even more amazing is that all this stuff was put into this baby before he was even born. Yeah, God creates every baby while he or she is being formed inside their mother. Each birth is a miracle of God's power!

ChallengePoint

Sometimes God's power is only thought of in relation to strength, oceans or waterfalls. Something as small and gentle as a newborn baby doesn't seem so powerful until you really stop and think about it. Look around you – the people you see each day began life as babies, knit together by God. What a powerful miracle!

Having Faith

God treats us much better than we deserve, and because of Christ Jesus, He freely accepts us and sets us free from our sins.

Romans 3:24

Faith is sometimes described as believing in something you can't explain or see. For example, when you sit down in a chair, you believe it will support you and not send you crashing to the floor.

Faith in God requires believing in His plan that forgives your sins and cleans up your heart. Salvation requires faith and trust in God. Do you trust Him enough to believe Him?

ChallengePoint

Learning to live by faith means learning to trust God in every situation. As you see Him work in one small way, your faith grows a little so you trust Him more the next time. Don't be discouraged if your faith wavers once in a while. It's a process to learn to trust Him. But it begins with the step of faith in trusting God for salvation – a fantastic, amazing, loving plan He made for you to free you from the price of your own sins.

Giving

On the first day of every week, each one of you should put aside money as you have been blessed. Save it up so you will not have to collect money after I come.

1 Corinthians 16:2

Things cost money. You spend money on things you need and things you want. It also costs money to do ministry. Those people who have been called into a career of serving God need to be supported; supplies for doing ministry such as books and study guides cost money; running a church costs money.

Those things are paid for by normal, everyday people giving some of their own money. This is God's instruction – to give money on each Lord's Day for God's work.

ChallengePoint

The cool thing about this giving instruction is this: people who have a normal, everyday job in their own town can have a part in reaching people for Christ around the world just by giving and supporting missionaries and church workers in other parts of the world. Cool, huh? Your offering can make a difference in someone's life on the other side of the world!

Abiding in Him

I sleep and wake up refreshed because You, Lord, protect me.

Psalm 3:5

When your family goes on a car trip, do you fall asleep in the back seat? If you do, you can sleep peacefully because you know your parents will take care of you. You know that they know where they are going and you have nothing to worry about.

That's what happens in all of life when you are abiding in God. You know He will take care of things. No matter what comes up, you know He can take care of it, so you can sleep peacefully and not be worried about things.

ChallengePoint

The peace that comes from abiding doesn't happen automatically, so don't get discouraged. It's a learning process to trust God enough not to worry about things. Don't get discouraged if you find you are still worrying once in a while, remind yourself that God is watching over you and that you can trust Him. Peace will come as you trust Him more.

Depend on the LORD in whatever you do, and your plans will succeed.

Proverbs 16:3

Does this mean that you can get whatever you want from God? You want to be a millionaire – BANG, you've got it! You want to be a professional ball player – BANG, it's yours! Yeah, that's not really what this verse means.

Look at the first phrase of the verse. It's important. Commit your actions to God. Pray about them, seek His guidance and know that you're doing what He wants you to do. Then you can trust Him to bless your actions, because you are doing what He wants you to do.

ChallengePoint

God is not a big Santa Claus in the sky who will give you whatever you want. He will bless your work and your efforts, but make sure you are doing what He wants you to do. Commit your actions to Him. Pray for His guidance. Thank Him for His blessings.

Using His Gifts

Whatever is good and perfect comes down to us from God our Father, who created all the lights in the heavens. He never changes or casts a shifting shadow.

James 1:17

This pretty much says it all – everything that you might consider good comes to you from God. He is the giver of all good gifts. So you can't take any credit for the things you have. No one can.

A person may work hard to achieve goals or to make money or to gain power ... but God is the one who makes it all possible. He is the giver of all things.

ChallengePoint

Some people puff up with pride as they think about all they have accomplished. They take all the credit for their success themselves. What they are forgetting is that ultimately everything comes from God. Yes, you may work very hard for success, but the opportunity, the strength to work, the brain to think ... all of it comes from God. Thank Him for His gifts and use them to the best of your ability.

His Love

For you are a people holy to the LORD your God. The LORD your God has chosen you out of all the peoples on the face of the earth to be His people, His treasured possession.

Deuteronomy 7:6

Do you own something that you consider to be your treasure? Something that is so special to you that you're sometimes amazed that you even own it? It is pretty cool to have something that special. It is even cooler to BE that special thing.

You are God's special treasure. He chose you. He didn't have to. He didn't need to have a special treasure – He's got all of creation. But He loves you so much that He considers you His treasure.

ChallengePoint

You have to admit that this is amazing. God ... the Creator of the universe ... the most powerful force anywhere ... loves you so much that He chose you as His special treasure. That's a lot of love. Doesn't that make you want to love Him back?

His Love

The Father has loved us so much that we are called children of God. And we really are His children. The reason the people in the world do not know us is that they have not known Him.

1 John 3:1

You don't get to choose your family. They don't get to choose you either if you're born into a family. You get what you get and, thankfully, it usually works out fine.

The awesome thing about God is that He "adopts" you into His family when you ask Jesus to be your Savior. He doesn't just say that you're on His team or that you are His friend. He calls you His child and He loves you as His child.

ChallengePoint

A father's love for his son is very deep and strong. It's a giving love that protects and guards. It's a love that wants to give as much as possible to his child. A father's love wants to teach and direct and help his son to grow into a mature young man. God's love for you is a father's love. Awesome.

Praying

Don't worry about anything, but pray about everything. With thankful hearts offer up your prayers and requests to God. Then, because you belong to Christ Jesus, God will bless you with peace that no one can completely understand. And this peace will control the way you think and feel.

Philippians 4:6-7

Don't worry. Right. Well, you wouldn't worry about anything at all if you knew that all you had to do was mention what you're worried about and BAM, someone would take care of it.

That's what you can do with God. You can tell Him anything and everything. He cares and He will help. The thing is that He doesn't always work on your time schedule or do what you think He should do. That's where the faith thing comes in. Tell Him what you need. Trust Him to take care of it.

ChallengePoint

It's the trusting and waiting that is sometimes hard, right? If you've been around God very long, you know you can tell Him anything and everything. But when He doesn't leap into action, well, the waiting gets difficult. So take it a step at a time and learn to wait in faith. It comes with practice.

Seeking His Protection

He will order His angels to protect you wherever you go.

Psalm 91:11

Famous people often have bodyguards to protect them from the crowds that surround them wherever they go. As fans approach a celebrity, a bodyguard seemingly appears from nowhere and steps between the fan and the star. The bodyguard is also the protector.

Do you think it would be cool to have a bodyguard? Well, you do ... kind of. God orders His angels to watch out for you and protect you wherever you go. You have a whole army of bodyguards watching out for you!

ChallengePoint

Did you ever wonder how often God protects you when you don't even know about it? An angel may move you over to protect you from danger, or grab your shoulder to keep you from falling ... you just don't know. But God knows. How cool is it to have His bodyguards taking care of you!

Seeking His Protection

Give all your worries to Him, because He cares about you.
1 Peter 5:7

Here's the formula:

1. Scary things happen to everyone: Parents get divorced; you have to change schools; you deal with serious illness. Scary things.
2. You can worry and fret so much that you're afraid to leave the house ... or ...
3. You can ask God to help you be strong enough to get through these things.
4. You ask ... He does. He protects your heart from the agony of worry and the temptation to turn away from Him.
5. Why? Because He loves you.

ChallengePoint

Bad things are going to happen. There's no way around that. How you handle them is up to you. Do you turn to God or worry yourself sick? Doesn't seem like a difficult choice, does it?

Knowing God by
Serving Him

Everything you were taught can be put into a few words:
Respect and obey God! This is what life is all about.

Ecclesiastes 12:13

You should serve God. Does that statement freak you out? Do you want to run through the house screaming, "I can't sing. I can't teach. I can't preach sermons. How can I serve God?" Serving God begins with two simple steps and they are outlined in this Scripture verse.

1. Respect God. This doesn't mean be scared silly of Him. It means honor Him with the respect that He deserves.
2. Obey His commands. First you have to know them. They're in the Bible, so reading the Bible is implied here. Then, make the choice each day to obey them.

ChallengePoint

These two steps are the first steps on the journey to serving God. You must respect Him and obey Him otherwise your relationship with Him is not worth much. Serve Him today, beginning with these two steps.

"Whoever wants to be a leader among you must be your servant."

Matthew 20:26

This Scripture verse turns the way the world looks at things upside down. A powerful leader would never be a servant. Instead, he would expect people to serve him. His "people" would do the boring jobs and the dirty work. His time would be saved for the "important things."

Jesus didn't agree. He washed His disciples' feet. That was servant's work. You are supposed to be like Jesus, so serving God means serving those around you.

ChallengePoint

Look for ways to serve others. Look for things to do for them that will let them know you care about them. Don't grumble about it. Don't brag about it. Just do it.

Serving Him

So, do not let sin control your life here on earth so that you do what your sinful self wants to do.

Romans 6:12

You have a choice:

- Go with the flow ... do what the crowd does ... do whatever you feel like.
  Or
- Rein your desires in. Just as a rider must control the reins of a horse in order to guide it, pull in the ideas and thoughts that pop into your mind. Put them through the filter of "What does God want me to do?"

ChallengePoint

You serve God by obeying Him. That filter in your heart and mind that asks, "What does God want me to do?" is a good monitor for your choices. Don't let sin rule your life. Choose to serve and obey God.

Obeying Him

We know that God accepts only those who have faith in Jesus Christ. No one can please God by simply obeying the Law. So we put our faith in Christ Jesus, and God accepted us because of our faith.

Galatians 2:16

You may have the idea of obedience pounded into your brain. But obeying God's laws isn't the actual goal. The really important thing is believing that Jesus, God's Son, came to earth and lived as a man, taught about knowing God, was killed by His enemies, dying willingly on the cross for your sins, was raised back to life by God, and now lives in heaven with Him.

Because of what He did, accepting Him as your Savior is what brings you into God's family. Obeying laws for the sake of obeying laws is not enough.

ChallengePoint

God does not just want your obedience. He wants you to be part of His family. Knowing Christ as Savior is the only way for that to happen. Obedience to God's laws grows from knowing Christ. It's a part of the journey to be like Him.

Obeying Him

The LORD has told you, human, what is good; He has told you what He wants from you: to do what is right to other people, love being kind to others, and live humbly, obeying your God.

Micah 6:8

When you play a game, whether it's a physical sport or a competitive board game, you have to know the rules. Once you know the rules, you can play the game, getting better at it the more you play. There's an old saying, "It's not whether you win or lose, it's how you play the game that matters." Playing by the rules is important. Obeying God falls under that same guideline. You have to know what to obey in order to obey. Get it? If you don't know the commands, you can't possibly obey. This verse gives you 3 simple steps in obeying: do what is right (you know that by knowing the rules in the Bible); love mercy (be kind, gentle and forgiving with others) and live humbly (submit to God and do what He wants).

ChallengePoint

Three simple steps. No, three steps that aren't always simple. But it's a starting point to know how to begin to obey God. It's a process to learn to obey more and more. But to begin, you must take the first step.

At the name of Jesus every knee should bow, in heaven and on earth and under the earth, and every tongue confess that Jesus Christ is Lord, to the glory of God the Father.

Philippians 2:10-11

Sometimes confession is admitting that you messed up. Sometimes confession is admitting that you know something or someone.

In these Scripture verses confession is admitting who Jesus is. This is not an easy thing for people in some parts of the world who might be kicked out of their families or even killed for admitting that they believe Jesus is Lord. This confession is important, though. It shows to the confessor, to the people listening and to God Himself that the person speaking it believes it.

ChallengePoint

If you knew you were going to be hurt for confessing your belief in God, would you do it anyway? God doesn't have much good to say about wishy-washy faith. If you believe in your heart, speak it with your mouth.

His Forgiveness

Blessed are they whose transgressions are forgiven, whose sins are covered.

Romans 4:7

God's forgiveness is not like any human forgiveness. When you mess up and hurt another person, you confess what you did and ask for forgiveness. Hopefully the person you wronged forgives you and your relationship is restored. But even when he has forgiven you it is often hard for the person to forget what you did. It kind of lurks there in the back of his mind.

It is not like that with God. He forgives and forgets – what you did is put out of sight. Forgotten. Over and done with.

ChallengePoint

God is so awesome. He forgives your sin and then forgets about it. He will never throw it back in your face again. It's over. You get to start fresh with a clean slate. God's forgiveness is wrapped up in His love for you.

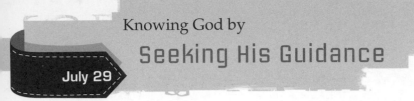

Knowing God by

Seeking His Guidance

July 29

You died to this life, and your real life is hidden with Christ in God.

Colossians 3:3

God's plan for you is very connected to Christ. If you want to know what His plans for your future are, you'd better get to know Christ better and better, because that's how you'll find out the plan. Christ is the nucleus of God's plan – everything revolves around Him.

Don't get the idea that God is trying to keep His plan a secret from you. He wants you to get to know Christ better, because His goal is for you to become more and more like Christ. So, getting to know Him means you learn how to be like Him ... which is God's plan for your life.

ChallengePoint

Sometimes people try to make things about God a lot more complicated than necessary. God isn't trying to keep secrets from you. He loves you. Christ is your model of how to live, so learning about Him answers the question of God's guidance in your life.

His Faithfulness

Those who trust the Lord will find new strength. They will be strong like eagles soaring upward on wings; they will walk and run without getting tired.

Isaiah 40:31

God's faithfulness is so evident in this Scripture verse. Trust Him and nothing can bring you down in this life. Trust Him and His strength will help you fly high. Trust Him and His strength will keep your strength coming. Trust Him and you will keep on keeping on.

This is God's promise to you and He always keeps His promises. God is faithful.

ChallengePoint

Does this mean you will never have problems? Nope. Does it mean that trusting will always be easy? Nope. Does it mean you will always fly high and stay energized? Nope. It means that God is faithful to be beside you; lifting you up when you fall, and strengthening you when you're weak. He is faithful to His promise to help you.

Celebrating Him

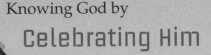

July 31

Praise the LORD! Praise God in His sanctuary; praise Him in His mighty heaven!

Psalm 150:1

Why is it important to celebrate God? There's a good answer to that question and it is this: If you are a typical person, much of your prayer time is spent asking God to do things for you. Of course, He wants to hear your prayers because He cares about the things that concern you.

But once in a while, He wants you to stop asking and start celebrating. Notice the things He has done for you in the past, the things He is doing right now, and the promises He has given you for the future. Celebrate His power, His strength and His love!

ChallengePoint

Wow, it's easy to get stuck in the "God, would You fix this" mode, isn't it? Try to balance your prayer time with celebrating God. Pay attention to all the wonderful things He does for you and gives you. Take time not to just say thanks, but to celebrate!

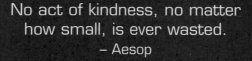

No act of kindness, no matter
how small, is ever wasted.
– Aesop

August

Knowing God by

Enduring

I can do all things through Christ, because He gives me strength.

Philippians 4:13

Endurance means you keep on going, working through problems, learning and growing. It means fighting through tiredness, injury or illness. It means you do not stop, ever, for any reason.

Endurance is a great characteristic to have. You see it a lot with successful athletes and businessmen who do not let much of anything stop them in the effort to get to the top. Something drives them to work that hard.

In the Christian life that kind of drive comes from Christ's strength inside you. He gives you the energy to keep on going, learning and growing.

ChallengePoint

When you live your life with Christ as your strength, the possibilities are endless. He will help you accomplish anything that He wants you to accomplish. Never give up and never stop trusting Him.

Knowing God by
Enduring

Control yourselves and be careful! The devil, your enemy, goes around like a roaring lion looking for someone to eat. Refuse to give in to him, by standing strong in your faith. You know that your Christian family all over the world is having the same kinds of suffering.

1 Peter 5:8-9

There is strength in knowing that you are not alone. The devil is trying to trip up everyone. He doesn't want anyone to follow God. He's always on the look out for someone he can attack.

This verse encourages you to endure – stand firm against the devil. You can only do that by being strong in your faith. God will help you by keeping you alert and giving you strength to fight off the devil's attacks.

ChallengePoint

It is so important to endure against the devil. Do not let him win. Do not even let him get a tiny little victory in your life. Fight him by being strong in your faith. Stay close to God and endure the attacks of the devil.

Being Like Christ

Our faces, then, are not covered. We all show the Lord's glory, and we are being changed to be like Him. This change in us brings ever greater glory, which comes from the Lord, who is the Spirit.

2 Corinthians 3:18

You can't reflect what you haven't seen. A mirror simply reflects what is right in front of it. It shows an exact image.

God, in His amazing grace, opens your eyes to see what Christ is like. Then His Spirit helps you reflect Christ's image. You become more and more like Him as you see Him and reflect Him. The Holy Spirit is what makes the reflecting and changing possible.

ChallengePoint

Again ... you can't reflect what you haven't seen ... so ask God's Spirit to show you more and more of what Christ is like. The more you see Him and understand Him, the more likely you are to be changed into His likeness. Be a mirror that reflects Christ's image back to God. What a pleasing image that is!

Being Like Christ

Don't use foul or abusive language. Let everything you say be good and helpful, so that your words will be an encouragement to those who hear them.

Ephesians 4:29

Words ... they can rip up a person's self-esteem. You do not ever read of Christ using foul or abusive language. Sure, He was firm sometimes – especially with those Pharisees – but when you read Christ's words, you see that while He was firm and honest, He always took the high road.

Christ also taught that the second most important commandment is to love others. Abusive language doesn't go with that, does it?

ChallengePoint

What is abusive language? Words that attack a person's character; words that attack a person's intelligence; words that attack pretty much anything. That kind of language is never good or helpful and is never an encouragement to others. Think about how the words you speak will land on another person's heart. Speak words that are positive and encouraging.

Being Like Christ

God loves you and has chosen you as His own special people. So be gentle, kind, humble, meek, and patient.

Colossians 3:12

Did you get that? God CHOSE you. He chose YOU! He chose you because He loves you. Since He loves you, He wants to help you become more and more like Christ.

He even gives you a list of characteristics right here that will make you more like Christ: Gentleness, kindness, humility, meekness and patience. Behaving in these ways will make you more like God.

ChallengePoint

These five characteristics are not easy to have every day. In fact, it's nearly impossible without God's help. Since He wants you to be like Christ, and since He chose you to be His child, He will help you develop these characteristics.

I love the Lord, for He heard my voice; He heard my cry for mercy.

Psalm 116:1

Part of the reason you love someone is because they bring out the best in you. Why do you love God? Can you list the things about Him that you appreciate the most?

This verse shows one of the ways God loves you. He hears your prayers. He cares about the things you care about and hears your cries for His help. That's one way you know God's love. He listens.

ChallengePoint

What things about God's love do you most appreciate? Different things mean a lot to different people. Think about the way God loves that means the most to you.

Knowing God by

Sharing Love

August 7

Even more than all this, clothe yourself in love. Love is what holds you all together in perfect unity.

Colossians 3:14

You get up in the morning and put on your clothes. You choose a shirt and pants to wear that make you look the way you want to look. A lot of kids tend to choose the same styles of clothes. Everyone kind of looks the same.

You have another choice of something to wear every day. Love. God is love and His Word tells you how important it is for all of His family to be wrapped in love as He is.

ChallengePoint

Love is what binds God's people together. It's the characteristic that shows you belong to God. Wear love every day in the way you treat other people. Thank God for His love for you.

Knowing God by

Showing Courage

August 8

I am proud of the good news! It is God's powerful way of saving all people who have faith, whether they are Jews or Gentiles. The good news tells how God accepts everyone who has faith, but only those who have faith. It is just as the Scriptures say, "The people God accepts because of their faith will live."

Romans 1:16-17

How strong is your belief in God? How courageous are you in taking a stand for Him? Are you willing to risk what people around you might think about you because you follow God?

It takes courage to let people know you are a Christian. It could mean that others make fun of you. It could mean that you choose not to do some things that other kids will do. Courage to share the story of God's love with others also gives others the chance to know Him.

ChallengePoint

Your courage to stand for God and to share His love with others is so important. It is the chance for others to learn about God. If others see that your faith in God means so much to you that you are courageous enough to share it, they may just listen.

Witnessing His Power

"I am the Alpha and the Omega – the beginning and the end," says the Lord God. "I am the One who is, who always was, and who is still to come – the Almighty One."

Revelation 1:8

Who was here in the beginning? God. He made everything there is. He created the world out of nothing. Who is here now? God. He walks beside you every day. He knows what will happen in your life before it even happens. He guides and protects you.

Who will be here in the future? God – One day He will bring His children to heaven and will defeat Satan and get rid of him forever. God's power is shown in His constant and forever presence.

ChallengePoint

So what should God's presence in the beginning, now, and in the future mean to you? When everything else that seems to be so powerful is gone … God will still be here. He is the only thing that will endure to the end and beyond. That gives you reason to trust Him and call on His power in your life.

Knowing God by
Giving

It doesn't matter how much you have. What matters is how much you are willing to give from what you have.

2 Corinthians 8:12

Giving to God's work is a privilege. It's a way of worshiping Him. The key is your attitude about giving. If you give grudgingly and wishing you didn't have to, then you aren't going to consider it a privilege or worship. If you give eagerly, glad to help and you're excited by the chance to be a part of His work, then you will be worshiping as you give.

Knowing you are a part of God's work because of your own generosity connects you with God's people around the world!

ChallengePoint

Attitude makes all the difference. Being a part of God's work in another part of the world is a privilege. Give with the right attitude and enjoy the blessing.

He mocks proud mockers but gives grace to the humble.

Proverbs 3:34

People who brag about themselves do not convince anyone of anything. The only people who think a bragger is awesome is the bragger himself. Remember that God's focus is that you love Him and love others.

Bragging about your own accomplishments, skills, brains, looks or anything else does not show much love to others. When you push down your own pride and lift others up by complimenting their successes, you are living the way God encourages you to live.

ChallengePoint

Some people brag about themselves because they want others to know what they have accomplished. But instead of doing that, they should be noticing others' successes and talents. Encourage them to use their skills and talents for God's work. Lift others up!

Knowing God by

Trusting Him

Since we have a great High Priest who rules over God's house, let us go right into the presence of God, with sincere hearts fully trusting Him. For our guilty consciences have been sprinkled with Christ's blood to make us clean, and our bodies have been washed with pure water.

Hebrews 10:21-22

Have you ever been called into the principal's office because you were in some kind of trouble? It's a scary feeling. You know you're in trouble and will probably be punished.

Do you feel that same kind of fear about coming into God's presence? You shouldn't if you trust the fact that God loves you. You know He does because He has made you clean from your sin by the blood of His own Son, Jesus.

ChallengePoint

Trusting God and His love and care for you takes away a lot of fear. Of course, you still respect Him and honor Him, but trust and fear don't live in the same place. If your heart is filled with trust for God, then fear of God will disappear.

Trusting Him

"Don't let your hearts be troubled. Trust in God, and trust in Me."

John 14:1

Anxiety. Fretting. Worry. Fear. This is one possible chain of emotions that happen when you don't trust God. Whatever causes your anxiety – a big exam at school, giving an oral book review, problems at home, parents splitting up, a major illness – leads to fretting.

Fretting means you can't get the issue off your mind. You're constantly trying to figure out how to "fix it." When you realize you can't fix it, then you worry about it. As the worry grows you get scared. Wow, exhausting, huh? That whole process can be avoided by ... trusting God.

ChallengePoint

When things are going great you may declare how much you trust God. But you don't really know if you trust Him until problems come. When things get tough, do you believe completely in His love and care for you? Do you believe He will take care of you and the situation, and that He always has your best interests in mind? That's trust.

Using His Gifts

Because of God you are in Christ Jesus, who has become for us wisdom from God. In Christ we are put right with God, and have been made holy, and have been set free from sin.

1 Corinthians 1:30

You've possibly seen movies about spies or secret agents who have incredible super-techno gadgets made for them that help them defeat the bad guys and always win. Wouldn't it be a boring (and short) story if the spy said, "No thanks, I don't need that super-techno gadget. I'll just fight on my own." Yeah, right. Whether you're a make-believe superhero, or a real-life soldier, or a professional athlete ... it just makes sense to use everything available to you to do your job better and make you safer.

Well, that's what you should do with God's gifts. He makes available His own wisdom, strength, power, holiness – everything about Himself – through Jesus.

ChallengePoint

God makes so much available to you ... do you accept and use it? The Christian life and living for God is so much easier if you accept God's gifts. Thank Him for them. Use them. Grow with them.

His Love

God shows His great love for us in this way: Christ died for us while we were still sinners.

Romans 5:8

Did you ever do something nice for someone even while he was being mean to you? You were kind to him in the hope that he would someday be kind to you.

Compare that act of kindness to God – He gave His only Son to humankind even while they were rejecting Him and disobeying Him.

He showed His incredible love for you even before you decided you loved Him and would obey Him. That's real love that is completely undeserved.

ChallengePoint

Since God loves you that much, what's your response to Him? His love is so deep, wide, strong and powerful that it's impossible to measure it. Does the generosity of His love for you cause you to want to love Him more?

Praying

Early the next morning, while it was still dark, Jesus woke and left the house. He went to a lonely place, where He prayed.

Mark 1:35

Just in case you think you've got life figured out and you think that means you don't need to connect with God every day ... this verse shows that you are wrong. You may be smart, wise and strong but if Jesus needed and wanted to pray every morning, then so do you.

This verse is just one example of how important prayer was to Jesus when He lived on earth. Even if he had spent a long day teaching and healing, surrounded by crowds of people who all wanted something from Him, He still focused on connecting with God, even if it meant getting up before sunrise to have time to do that.

ChallengePoint

Jesus is your example of how to live for God. For Him prayer – conversation with God – was very important. So the model for you is to also make prayer very important. Start every day by connecting with God and asking for His guidance and help throughout the day.

His Love

May you have the power to understand how wide, how long, how high, and how deep His love is. May you experience the love of Christ, though it is too great to understand fully. Then you will be made complete with all the fullness of life and power that comes from God. Now all glory to God who is able to accomplish infinitely more than we might ask or think.

Ephesians 3:18-20

There are some mysteries that are just too big. You will never understand them in this life. The magnitude of God's love is one of those things. It's so big and so complete that it's impossible to comprehend. Yet, God wants you to experience it more and more so that you understand it better and better.

His love gives you power – His power – to live life to the fullest. His love gives power to do more things for Him than you could have ever dreamed.

ChallengePoint

How do you begin to understand God's love more? By experiencing it and acknowledging it in your life. Spend some time each day thinking about what He has given you that day. Think about the ways He shows His love to you. Think about the things He helps you accomplish.

The LORD is good. He protects those who trust Him in times of trouble.

Nahum 1:7

The safest place to run to is God. Some places where you try to find protection – with friends, hobbies and activities – will cave in when things get tough.

God will not. He will protect you from anything and everything. All you have to do is come to Him and trust Him to take care of you.

ChallengePoint

The trusting might be the hard part here. God doesn't promise to keep you from troubles. But He does promise to be with you whatever troubles come. Sometimes the temptation is to turn and run when problems get bigger instead of smaller. Fight that temptation. Stay close to God and let Him guide you through the hard times. Ask Him to make you stronger from your problems.

Knowing God by
Serving Him

August 19

"If you give even a cup of cold water to one of the least of My followers, you will surely be rewarded."

Matthew 10:42

Serving God can be the simplest of things. Sometimes you think you can only serve Him by being a minister, a missionary, a Bible teacher or somehow being in full-time Christian work.

In reality, serving God is just paying attention to people around you. Noticing what they need and thinking about how you can help them. Something as easy and simple as offering a drink of water to someone who is thirsty.

ChallengePoint

God just wants you to pay attention to people around you. Don't get so caught up in your own life or problems that you only think about yourself. Serve God by looking around and seeing what simple thing you can do to show someone else that you care ... and that God cares.

Serving Him

God is good. So I beg you to offer your bodies to Him as a living sacrifice, pure and pleasing. That's the most sensible way to serve God. Don't be like the people of this world, but let God change the way you think. Then you will know how to do everything that is good and pleasing to Him.

Romans 12:1-2

In the 2008 Olympics a young swimmer named Michael Phelps amazed everyone by winning eight gold medals. Three medals were from relay races. Michael (and his relay team-mates) had all given their entire lives and bodies to getting ready for their races. They practiced for hours, ate high-calorie diets, and got plenty of rest. Their focus was preparing to win their races.

The effort to serve God should be just as intense. God doesn't ask for just an hour a week, He asks for your entire body and mind to be given to Him.

ChallengePoint

Being that focused on serving God changes the way you think. It changes the way you live. After a while you are changed. You don't live like the people who are not serving God. You don't think the way they think or act the way they act. Your life is defined by service to God.

Obeying Him

"If you love Me, you will do what I have said, and My Father will love you. I will also love you and show you what I am like."

John 14:21

There's an old saying, "If it walks like a duck, looks like a duck, and quacks like a duck, then it must be a duck." This applies to obeying God. If you obey His commands it will show in the way you live and the way you speak. If you don't obey them, that will show too.

The more you obey Him, the more you will learn about Him. You get to learn more as you show Him that you are obeying what you do know.

ChallengePoint

You can't obey what you don't know, so read His Word to find out how you should be living. The first step to obeying God is knowing Him.

Knowing God by
Obeying Him

You have accepted Christ Jesus as your Lord. Now keep on following Him.

Colossians 2:6

God has such high ambitions for you. That's why He says that accepting Jesus isn't the end of the journey for you. If you continue to follow Him, you will learn so much more about living for Him and there is such joy in that.

How do you follow Jesus?

1. Read God's Word. You'll learn God's commands for your life from it. You'll also see how Jesus lived on this earth. How He interacted with others and how He honored God.
2. Pray. Talk to God and then be quiet and listen for Him to speak to your heart.

ChallengePoint

Two simple steps = big rewards.

Confessing Sin

Anyone whose name was not found recorded in the Book of Life was thrown into the lake of fire.

Revelation 20:15

God takes confession very seriously. Confession, which is admitting your sins to God, shows that you are willing to be honest with God. Part of confessing is asking for God's forgiveness.

If you don't trust God enough to confess, then you must question whether your relationship with Him is real. If it's not real then you will never join God in heaven. When you leave this earth, you will be thrown into the lake of fire with Satan. God takes confession seriously.

ChallengePoint

Confession is an important part of your relationship with God. Make it part of your daily talk with Him. Confess wrong thoughts, actions and attitudes. Ask forgiveness and for His help in correcting those things.

His Forgiveness

"I promise you that any of the sinful things you say or do can be forgiven, no matter how terrible those things are. But if you speak against the Holy Spirit, you can never be forgiven. That sin will be held against you forever."

Mark 3:28-29

Just in case you think you have been so bad that God could never forgive you – or would even want to – this Scripture verse sets that straight. Any sin can be forgiven, even being disrespectful to God. He wants to forgive you and is willing to forgive pretty much everything.

However, don't feel that His willingness to forgive gives you the freedom to do whatever you want. God does have a bottom line.

ChallengePoint

God's bottom line is disrespecting the Holy Spirit and His power and work in your life. Think before you speak about Him. Pay attention to your attitudes. Otherwise, confess your sins to God and believe that He will forgive.

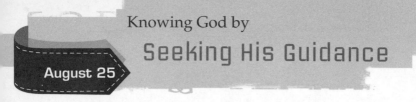

When people's steps follow the LORD, God is pleased with their ways.

Psalm 37:23

The bottom line here is: Don't wait for God to guide you if you aren't submitting to Him. That means this: God wants to guide your steps. He will guide you, but not if you haven't asked Jesus into your heart and then sought God's guidance.

Obey the knowledge you have; the commands you know; then seek God's guidance in other areas of life.

ChallengePoint

Some commands are very clear, the Ten Commandments for example. If you aren't making any attempts to obey the commands you have, then don't bother to ask for guidance in other things. Guidance comes in steps … do your part.

Being Like Christ

If you do the right thing, honesty will be your guide. But if you are crooked, you will be trapped by your own dishonesty.

Proverbs 11:3

Sometimes it seems like the good guys lose and the bad guys win, doesn't it? People who are dishonest seem to keep getting ahead. The more rotten things they do, the more successful they are. It's frustrating!

Well, have faith, because these people will eventually get what's coming to them. Being like Christ means being guided by honesty and treating others in the way you would like to be treated. People who are consistently dishonest will one day have to answer for that – to God.

ChallengePoint

Dishonesty; cheating others and lying to them, is as unlike Christ as you can get. All people will one day stand before God to be judged, and that dishonesty will be answered for then, if not before. Live like Christ – guided by honesty.

Then Christ will make His home in your hearts as you trust in Him. Your roots will grow down into God's love and keep you strong.

Ephesians 3:17

Christ is at home in your heart. Cool, huh? Hopefully it's cool. Are you making your heart a comfortable place for Him to be? Are your actions and thoughts things you want Him to know about? They better be since He's there all the time.

He will help you be more and more obedient. As you trust Him more and more, your understanding of God's love will grow deeper and you will be stronger.

ChallengePoint

Since He lives in your heart Christ is with you all the time. You probably like that when you have needs you want Him to take care of. But this verse is a good reminder during the times when you might be just as happy if He wasn't around. He is. Live your life in a way that pleases and honors Him.

For our high priest is able to understand our weaknesses.
He was tempted in every way that we are, but He did not
sin.

Hebrews 4:15

OK, you cannot say that God doesn't understand things
like the guys telling dirty jokes and wanting you to join
in. You can't say He doesn't understand the temptation
to cheat; or the urge to tell a lie to protect yourself. He
understands.

This verse tells you that Christ had the same kinds of
temptations to protect Himself and promote Himself as
you do. Read about Satan tempting Him in Matthew 4.
He understands. He's been through it.

ChallengePoint

How cool is it that God knows and understands what
you struggle with. He can help you because He does
understand. He will help you stand strong – just as
Christ did when He faced heavy temptation.

Loving Him

Love the L<small>ORD</small> your God with all your heart, all your soul, and all your strength.

Deuteronomy 6:5

God loves you completely. From the simple little chorus you learned as a child, "Jesus loves me this I know; for the Bible tells me so" to heavy-duty verses such as John 3:16 you know that He holds nothing back.

He gives everything to you. His focus is you. His Word says that He considers you His masterpiece. He asks that you love Him back just as completely and intently.

ChallengePoint

Love Him with all your heart, soul and strength. That means that nothing at all comes before Him. He is the most important to you. It means that nothing comes between you and your desire to serve Him and know Him better. Nothing.

Loving Others

May the Lord make your love grow more and multiply for each other and for all people so that you will love others as we love you.

1 Thessalonians 3:12

Some people are hard to like, let alone love. That's just the way it is and pretty much everyone agrees with that statement. However, God says it's important to Him that you love others – not just your family and friends – but all people.

That's not easy. But look at the first phrase of this verse: "May the Lord make ..." How cool is that! God will help you as you strive to love all people. It's important to Him, so He will help!

ChallengePoint

God knows that certain people are hard to love. He knows that as you look around the world, certain cultures may be hard for other cultures to love. But it matters to Him that people love each other more and more. So He will help. If you have trouble loving one person or a whole country full of people – ask Him to help you with that. He will.

Showing Courage

Put on every piece of God's armor to resist the enemy in the time of evil. Then after the battle you will still be standing firm.

Ephesians 6:13

Different pieces of armor protect different parts of the body. God has provided exactly the armor you need to resist the devil's attacks on you. You can be courageous as you fight off Satan if you use what God has provided.

God doesn't expect you to fight this sneaky enemy in your own strength. Your courage can come from knowing you aren't alone – and because you use the armor God provides.

ChallengePoint

Everything you need to fight Satan is provided by God. Read Ephesians 6 to learn about the parts of the armor that will help you win each battle. Put the armor on and courageously stand strong!

It's not whether you win
or lose, its how you
play the game.
– Grantland Rice

September

Suppressing Our Pride

"For whoever exalts himself will be humbled, and whoever humbles himself will be exalted."

Matthew 23:12

You brag about yourself and how awesome, smart, athletic, and wonderful you are ... you're going down.

You point attention at others and how awesome, smart, athletic, and wonderful they are ... you're on your way to the top. Simple.

ChallengePoint

God's focus is always, always others. Lift others up. Encourage others. Love others. If you're busy bragging about yourself you won't be helping anyone else. Please God by encouraging others, not by bragging about yourself.

Those who go to God Most High for safety will be protected by the Almighty.

Psalm 91:1

It's a hot summer's day ... really hot ... you and your buddies go to play baseball at the park. The sun beats down on you with such vengeance that even while you're standing still perspiration is running down your face. You look around for something to give you shade to stand in. When you find something, you have to go to it. Being close to it gives you shade, then you can rest from the heat.

That's the way it is with God. When you stay close to Him – in the shelter of His presence, then you can rest. As long as you're in His shadow you know you're safe.

ChallengePoint

Being in God's shadow means you are close to Him, and that's the safest place to be.

Knowing God by

Trusting Him

September 3

Blessed are those who trust in the LORD and have made the LORD their hope and confidence.

Jeremiah 17:7

Being blessed means being very happy and having good fortune. That's what you get from trusting God completely.

Just as horses sometimes wear blinders that keep their vision focused on what is right in front of them, you should keep your focus directly on God and pleasing and obeying Him. That leads to trust, which leads to being blessed.

ChallengePoint

Trusting God completely leads to good things in your life. By trusting Him a little you learn to trust Him more the next time a problem comes up. More trust leads to more confidence and a better understanding of how much God loves you.

Using His Gifts

"Only people who don't know God are always worrying about such things. Your Father in heaven knows that you need all these. But more than anything else, put God's work first and do what He wants. Then the other things will be yours as well."

Matthew 6:32-33

People who don't know God have to worry about how to get everything themselves. They have to be concerned about protection, power and success.

As God's child, you don't really need to worry about that stuff. God knows what you need. He will take care of you. Your concern is to get to know Him and live in obedience to Him.

ChallengePoint

Knowing God does not guarantee that you will be rich or famous. Don't try to make this verse mean that. God will supply what you need (not want), but then you must live obediently for Him. Seek Him.

Knowing God by

His Love

As high as the sky is above the earth, so great is His love for those who respect Him.

Psalm 103:11

Go outside on a dark night and look up at the stars. The farthest star is millions of miles away from earth. God's love for you is bigger than that distance.

Look around at the hundreds of stars you can see in the sky. The night sky looks endless, doesn't it? God's love is bigger. It can't be measured. He loves you very, very much!

ChallengePoint

Respect and honor God in order to know His massive, constant love. He wants you to. He does!

Knowing God by
Praying

The LORD is close to all who call on Him, yes, to all who call on Him in truth.

Psalm 145:18

Be a gentleman." Have you heard that instruction before? When your parents say that, they usually mean you must be a little quieter, let someone else go first, don't be pushy and be more polite.

Jesus is a gentleman. He doesn't push His way into your life. He doesn't bang you on the head to get control. He waits for you to ask. He hopes you will, but He waits. When you do, He is right there to help, guide, give wisdom and bless you.

ChallengePoint

Prayer is an amazing privilege – the right to talk to God. He came up with this plan and hopes that you will take advantage of it in order to know Him better and to experience His closeness to you.

Seeking His Protection

I pray that God will take care of all your needs with the wonderful blessings that come from Christ Jesus!

Philippians 4:19

Whatever you need, God will supply. That's the promise of this verse. Notice, however, that it says "need", not "want." God will take care of you.

Wow, sometimes you may not be able to see how He will help you. Often God brings what you need right at the last minute or even in ways you don't recognize at the time. The key is He promises to take care of you.

ChallengePoint

Trust is so important here. Do you trust God to take care of you? Really? Even if things look hopeless? Even if it seems as though He isn't paying any attention to you? It is very important to trust Him as you seek His protection.

Knowing God by
Serving Him

"The master was full of praise. 'Well done, my good and faithful servant. You have been faithful in handling this small amount, so now I will give you many more responsibilities. Let's celebrate together!'"

Matthew 25:21

Let's look at this situation:

- You're given a little chore to do – it doesn't seem very important.
- You work hard and do your very best.
- Your parents are impressed with your work. They trust you, so they give you a more important chore.

This applies to what you do for God too. Hard work is rewarded. Do a little thing for God and He will trust you with more.

ChallengePoint

Serving God is a privilege. It's amazing that God allows people to partner with Him in His work on earth. If you work hard at the first small job God gives you, He will trust you with a bigger job the next time.

Do not follow foolish stories that disagree with God's truth, but train yourself to serve God. Training your body helps you in some ways, but serving God helps you in every way by bringing you blessings in this life and in the future life, too.

1 Timothy 4:7-8

Some people just like to argue. They want everyone to know that their ideas are best or that they are in control. It's easy to get caught up in arguments with them. But it gets you nowhere. A person like that will seldom listen to others' ideas or thoughts.

God says that instead of arguing, train yourself to be more controlled. Listen rather than argue, be more Godlike in how you relate to others.

ChallengePoint

Arguing is easy. Being quiet is not. Training to be more like God takes some effort, just like training your muscles to be stronger. Make the effort, though, and you will be a better servant of God.

Knowing God by
Obeying Him

The good or bad that children do shows what they are like.

Proverbs 20:11

Never, ever say that it doesn't matter to God what you do or say just because you're a kid. It's not true. God cares about your obedience from day one.

The minute you're born, the minute you accept Christ as Savior, He hopes that you will choose to obey Him. It makes a difference in your relationship with Him – yes, even as a kid.

ChallengePoint

Remember that other kids your age may listen to what you say about God's love even more than they would listen to an adult. Remember too, that they will be watching how you live to see if what you do matches what you say about your relationship with Him. Obedience and serving go together!

When people keep on sinning, it shows that they belong to the devil, who has been sinning since the beginning. But the Son of God came to destroy the works of the devil.

1 John 3:8

Obeying is not a one-time thing. You can choose to obey one day and think you're doing pretty good ... but then you have to do the same thing tomorrow, and the next day and the next.

If you don't choose to obey each day then you keep on sinning ... just like the devil does. Obeying God, even wanting to obey Him, shows that you're in God's family. You belong to Him.

ChallengePoint

It would be nice if you could flip a switch and always obey. But it doesn't work that way. The devil is going to do his best to keep you from obeying God, so you have to make a conscious choice several times a day to obey and not sin in order to show that you belong to God.

Confessing Sin

Create in me a pure heart, O God, and renew a steadfast spirit within me.

Psalm 51:10

When your sneakers are covered with mud you have to scrape the mud off, then wash them to get them clean. There isn't any other way. When your heart is dirty because it's filled with sin, it has to be cleaned too.

How? Confess your sin to God – admit it. Tell Him you know that what you did was wrong. Ask Him to clean your heart and help you be more obedient to Him.

ChallengePoint

Sometimes you may not even know what you need to confess. Then ask God to show you what your sins are. That's a good way to learn where your weaknesses are so that you can ask God to help you in those areas.

Knowing God by

His Forgiveness

Yet now He has reconciled you to Himself through the death of Christ in His physical body. As a result, He has brought you into His own presence, and you are holy and blameless as you stand before Him without a single fault.

Colossians 1:22

OK, how many times do you figure you've disobeyed God? Like a million? Yeah, it's more than a few times, right?

But look at what this Scripture verse says – when you stand before God, He will not hold a single fault against you – not even one! When He forgives your sin, He also forgets it. He will not bring it up to you at some time in the future.

ChallengePoint

This complete forgiveness is possible because of Christ's death for your sins. His death washed you clean and made forgiveness possible after you have asked Christ to be your Savior.

Seeking His Guidance

Fools think they are doing right, but the wise listen to advice.

Proverbs 12:15

This is basic information:

Insist that your way is the only way and you are a fool. You miss out on the experiences and wisdom of others who want to help you make good decisions.

A smart guy listens to others and learns from them. Of course, the best Person to listen to is God. You can't go wrong by seeking guidance from Him.

ChallengePoint

Don't be so arrogant that you think your way is the only way. Remember that God sees the big picture of your whole life. He truly is the only One who knows what is best for you.

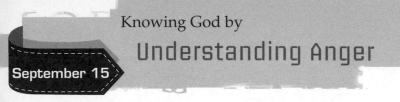

Knowing God by

Understanding Anger

September 15

In the same way, the tongue is a small thing that makes grand speeches.

James 3:5

When you lose your temper you can end up saying mean things just to hurt the person you're mad at. That's never a good idea. Controlling what you say is sometimes so hard.

But looking at anger through the filter of God's command to love others means you better control what you say!

ChallengePoint

If you let anger take control of you, more than likely you will say things that you'll regret later. Words come out that have no purpose other than hurting other people. There's no future in that and little evidence of God's love. Watch it. Keep your anger under control.

Knowing God by
His Faithfulness

God, Your thoughts are precious to me. They are so many!
If I could count them, they would be more than all the
grains of sand. When I wake up, I am still with You.

Psalm 139:17-18

Seriously ... walk along the beach and just think how many zillion grains of sand are on that beach. Can you count them? No, don't even go there.

But look at all those grains of sand and think about this: God thinks about you more often than that number of grains of sand. That means you are NEVER out of His thoughts – NEVER!

ChallengePoint

God is thinking about you all the time. You are never out of His thoughts. That's faithfulness – He is committed to you by thinking about you all the time and caring about you every moment.

Seeking Salvation

If anyone belongs to Christ, there is a new creation. The old things have gone; everything is made new!

2 Corinthians 5:17

Did you ever wish you could say some magic words and become a whole new person? You could be taller or stronger or smarter. Great idea, huh?

Well, God's salvation changes everything for you. You do become a new person when you ask Christ into your life. Salvation changes everything. You become a new person whose focus is obeying God and living for Him. Who you were before is gone!

ChallengePoint

You become a new person when you ask Christ into your life. He gets rid of the old stuff that made you disobedient to God. Your new life is obedient and loving and willing to serve ... no matter what!

Celebrating Him

Always be full of joy in the Lord. I say it again – rejoice!
Philippians 4:4

This may seem nearly impossible – ALWAYS be joyful? However, you need to understand that joy and happiness are two different things.

This verse doesn't say to always be happy. Happiness is based on circumstances – what's going on in your life. Joy is based on trust. It's a state of mind because you know God is in control. You know you can trust Him and you know that He loves you.

ChallengePoint

When you are full of joy in the Lord you can't help but celebrate Him. Just being in that state of mind reminds you of His amazing love for you. You'll constantly be thinking of all He does for you and how He cares for you. Those are all great things to celebrate!

> *Three times I begged the Lord to make this suffering go away. But He replied, "My kindness is all you need. My power is strongest when you are weak." So if Christ keeps giving me His power, I will gladly boast about how weak I am.*
>
> *2 Corinthians 12:8-9*

Learning a new level of math. Perfecting a new skill in gymnastics. Moving and having to go to a new school and make new friends. Missing your dad after a divorce.

Those are all difficult things to go through. At some point you might just beg God to take the pain away and let things be the way they used to be. The apostle Paul knew what that was like – but he had endurance and God blessed him by giving him the strength to keep on going.

ChallengePoint

It's only when things are tough that you find out if you have the strength and power to endure. If you call on God for strength to keep on going, He will give it to you and you will be blessed.

Being Like Christ

Let your roots grow down into Him, and let your lives be built on Him. Then your faith will grow strong in the truth you were taught, and you will overflow with thankfulness.

Colossians 2:7

Tree roots go deep into the earth and get the nutrition and water the tree needs to grow. In the same way, if your roots go down deep into Christ, your nutrition and water will come from Him. That means you'll be feeding your spirit and your heart with healthy stuff and you will grow stronger.

Christ wants to help you grow strong in your faith. He will do whatever you will allow Him to do to help you.

ChallengePoint

God wants the best for you and that will come from letting Christ be your food and water. Learn to be like Him by learning from Him.

Keep on loving each other as brothers. Do not forget to entertain strangers, for by so doing some people have entertained angels without knowing it. Remember those in prison as if you were their fellow prisoners, and those who are mistreated as if you yourselves were suffering.

Hebrews 13:1-3

Thinking outside yourself is the beginning of being like Christ. Loving others and being kind – even to strangers – and paying attention to people who are in trouble.

That means noticing those who are sort of undesirable – people you might not want to associate with. People who were dirty, sick or in trouble never bothered Christ. He loved them all.

ChallengePoint

Becoming more like Christ means thinking of others and their needs before your own. It means getting out of your comfort zone and becoming friends with people who are way different from you. Can you do that?

Loving Him

Be very careful to obey all the commands and the instructions that Moses gave to you. Love the LORD your God, walk in all His ways, obey His commands, hold firmly to Him, and serve Him with all your heart and all your soul.

Joshua 22:5

Did you ever jump into a swimming pool and try to keep one part of your body dry? Like, hold one arm above the water and see if you could keep it from getting splashed? Yeah, that makes swimming not so much fun. You can't do much in the water if you're trying to stay dry.

That's how God's love is – if you're not going to jump in with both feet and let your whole body love Him back, then you're missing out on lots.

ChallengePoint

God loves you completely. Love Him back completely. Don't hold anything out.

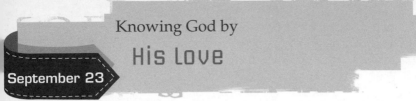

The Lord disciplines those He loves, and He punishes everyone He accepts as His child.

Hebrews 12:6

No one likes to be punished, right? You may have heard your parents say that when they have to punish you it hurts them more than it hurts you. Well, that's true, believe it or not.

It's also true of God. He doesn't enjoy punishing you but He does it because He loves you. If He didn't care at all about whether you learn and mature then He wouldn't bother with punishing you. He'd just let you do whatever. But He does care. You are His child and He loves you.

ChallengePoint

OK, being punished is not fun at all. But if you can view God's discipline and punishment as what He does because He loves you and wants to help you become a stronger Christian, does that make it easier? Unfortunately, being punished is about the best way you learn. Thank God for caring enough to punish you.

Showing Courage

*So do not be ashamed to tell people about our Lord Jesus,
and do not be ashamed of me, in prison for the Lord. But
suffer with me for the Good News. God, who gives us the
strength to do that, saved us and made us His holy people.*

2 Timothy 1:8-9

Courage shows the depth of your commitment. In other
words, if your belief in God is deep and strong, you'll
be courageous in telling others about it. You won't be
ashamed to take a stand for Him.

Your courage can come from God's strength. He'll
give you the power you need. Be sure, though, 'cause life
can get tough sometimes when you take a stand for Him.

ChallengePoint

There's no riding the fence on this. Be courageous and
take a stand for God. When you do, expect to pay for it –
Satan will want to slow you down. But turn to God for
strength and even more courage!

Knowing God by

Witnessing His Power

The voice of the LORD echoes above the sea. The God of glory thunders. The LORD thunders over the mighty sea. The voice of the LORD is powerful; the voice of the LORD is majestic.

Psalm 29:3-4

Does loud mean powerful? Not necessarily, but it sure gets people's attention, doesn't it? Look at how God's power is described – His voice is louder than the sea. It's powerful and full of majesty.

Sounds like it commands attention. Sounds like God's voice shows His power. You'd probably listen when you heard it.

ChallengePoint

God's power is not seen only in things such as thunderstorms or massive waterfalls. It's seen in the miracle of a newborn baby and in the simplicity of a flower. God's voice is powerful and the entire world will listen when He speaks. One day everyone will fall to their knees at the sound of His voice. Do you honor His power right now?

Abiding in Him

The world and everything that people want in it are passing away, but the person who does what God wants lives forever.

1 John 2:17

What are you grabbing onto? Where do you spend your time? What is most important to you? What do you want most in this world?

If each of those questions had an answer other than "Living for God" then you've got a problem. Living for God and obeying Him by sticking close to Him is abiding in Him. That should be most important in your life.

ChallengePoint

Nothing else in this world will last forever. Only God. Stick close to Him. Make Him the most important thing in your life. In the end that's all you will have.

Trusting Him

You make our hearts glad because we trust You, the only God.

Psalm 33:21

Can you celebrate when you're worried? Not with a lot of enthusiasm or energy. Can you party when you're afraid? Not too easily, 'cause you're worried about the danger.

What that means is that trusting God completely gives you the freedom to feel real joy. You know you don't have to worry about anything because you can trust Him. So you can relax and rejoice.

ChallengePoint

Trust does not come easily. It's a process to learn to trust God all the time, in any situation. But look at the joy that comes from trusting. That makes it worth starting the process, right?

Knowing God by

His Love

"I loved you as the Father loved Me. Now remain in My love."

John 15:9

The Bible is filled with stories of God's love for His Son, Jesus. He loved Jesus enough to raise Him back to life after He was killed. He had a plan for Jesus' life and that shows His love.

Jesus loves you as much as God loves Him. He passes the love along. He encourages you to stay close to Him and enjoy that love.

ChallengePoint

God's love is bottomless. He loves you more than you can imagine. Stay close to Him – enjoy His love.

Praying

So let us come boldly to the throne of our gracious God. There we will receive His mercy, and we will find grace to help us when we need it most.

Hebrews 4:16

You can come boldly to God with your requests because you know He loves you. You know He wants the best for you. You know that He wants to hear your requests. He wants to forgive your sins. He wants to help you in your life.

You don't have to beg Him. You don't have to sneak up on Him. You don't have to be shy about talking with Him.

ChallengePoint

Boldly come to God with your praises and your requests. He loves you and wants you to come to Him.

Seeking His Protection

Cast your cares on the LORD and He will sustain you; He will never let the righteous fall.

Psalm 55:22

You wouldn't go to a two-year-old and ask him to protect you and take care of you. What could he do? You wouldn't even go to a five-year-old and ask that. Nope, if you're going to ask someone to protect you and take care of your problems, you want to know for sure that he can do it.

The best One to ask for that kind of protection is God Himself. He has power over everything and ... He loves you.

ChallengePoint

God promises to take care of the godly. That means He will take care of those people who love, trust and seek to obey Him. Take steps along that pathway and then give your problems to God. He will take care of you. That's a promise!

God has big dreams for
every one of His children,
no matter how little they are!
– Anonymous

October

Serving Him

O LORD, You are my God; I will exalt You and praise Your name, for in perfect faithfulness You have done marvelous things, things planned long ago.

Isaiah 25:1

How can you serve God? Simple. Use your voice to praise Him. That means saying out loud how awesome He is and what incredible things He does.

Use your life to honor Him. That means making choices in how you live and how you speak that will show others that you respect Him and desire to obey Him.

ChallengePoint

These steps toward serving God are a journey. Some days you will succeed. Some days you will fail. But keep moving in the direction of serving God with your voice and your life.

But be holy in all you do, just as God, the One who called you, is holy.

1 Peter 1:15

Be holy. What does that mean? Holy means "to be set apart." So, if you're holy you are set apart from the rest of the world to do God's work. You have a different purpose than people who do not know God.

Serving God by being holy means being willing to do whatever God wants – regardless of what people around you are doing.

ChallengePoint

OK, admittedly this is not always easy. Your friends may give you a hard time. They may make fun of you. They may question you. But ultimately, they will notice that serving God is the most important thing in your life. That's a good thing.

Obeying Him

Oh, the joys of those who do not follow the advice of the wicked, or stand around with sinners, or join in with mockers.

Psalm 1:1

This is basic:

1. Obeying God is the most important thing.
2. Obeying God is not going to happen if you take advice from people who don't care about Him.
3. If you hang out with people who don't care about God, you probably won't be obeying God.
4. Don't hang out with people who don't obey God.

ChallengePoint

It can't get any simpler than that, can it? Obeying God is a choice you make every day (many times a day in fact). Get your advice about life from people who obey God. That's the only way you'll keep going in the right direction.

Obeying Him

From heaven God shows how angry He is with all the wicked and evil things that sinful people do to crush the truth.

Romans 1:18

God is not wishy-washy. Yes, He loves you. Yes, He wants the best for you. Yes, He gives second, third, fourth and fiftieth chances for obedience. But He has a bottom line.

When someone's actions of disobedience shuts down the truth being shared with others, God gets angry ... and He shows it. You don't want to see that.

ChallengePoint

No, you don't want God's anger to be directed at you. God is patient and He gives many chances for obedience. But He gets angry if your disobedience causes others to be unable to hear the truth of His love.

Obeying Him

In the same way, faith by itself – that does nothing – is dead.

James 2:17

Trusting God is important. Believing He loves you is important. But this faith isn't enough to be considered obedience.

Your faith needs to show in your life by the things you do and the words you speak. You can say all the "churchy" words you know, but if your actions don't match your words, you are not obeying.

ChallengePoint

Don't bother spouting Bible verses or speaking "churchy" words if your actions are not matching. The two need to go together – your words of faith and your actions. That shows real obedience.

Confessing Sin

Confess your sins to each other and pray for each other so God can heal you. When a believing person prays, great things happen.

James 5:16

Why would God tell you to confess your sins to people? Kind of a stinky thing to do, huh? Yeah, sometimes.

But think about this: Confessing to another person builds a family relationship. That person can help you not to keep doing the same sins. He can hold you accountable and he can pray for you.

ChallengePoint

Of course you don't go around confessing your sins to any Joe Schmo you meet. You choose a mature Christian who can give you good advice and who will actually pray for you. Maybe your friend confesses to you too, and you pray for him. The Christian life is not meant to be lived alone. God wants people to help each other.

Knowing God by

His Forgiveness

October 7

Even before He made the world, God loved us and chose
us in Christ to be holy and without fault in His eyes.

Ephesians 1:4

His mind was made up. Long before you were even born, God had already decided that when you asked for His forgiveness, He would give it to you. Before He even made the world, He had already decided that you were His child.

So whatever you throw at Him now, He will forgive ... because He loves you.

ChallengePoint

There's a confidence in this, isn't there? You know that there will be times when you mess up. There will even be times when you choose to disobey (bad choice by the way) but God already has forgiven you. Wow ... that's love!

Seeking His Guidance

You know where I go and where I lie down. You know everything I do.

Psalm 139:3

God has a plan. That is so awesome. He has a plan for your life. He has a plan for what you do, where you go to school, who you marry, where you live and what your future job is.

Do you find that comforting or scary? Don't worry. Remember, He loves you so His plan will make you happy and be the absolute best for you.

ChallengePoint

How do you find out what God's plan is? Ask Him. Read His Word and pray. Try to pay attention to the opportunities you get and notice what you really, really enjoy doing. He'll guide you 'cause He wants you to know.

Understanding Anger

October 9

Those who bring trouble on their families inherit the wind.
The fool will be a servant to the wise.

Proverbs 11:29

With whom do you most often fight or argue? Come on, be honest. If you have brothers or sisters, the answer is probably that you most often get angry with them. It makes sense when you think about it – you live with them, share space with them and are most comfortable letting your feelings show with them.

But God says to rein that anger in. Don't bring trouble on your family by letting your anger run free. That would make you look foolish.

ChallengePoint

What does "inherit the wind" mean? It means you have nothing. Everything that really matters is blown away by your anger. If you have anger issues ask God to help you control it and help you to be patient and forgiving with your family.

Knowing God by
His Faithfulness

Jesus Christ is the same yesterday, today, and forever.

Hebrews 13:8

Dependability. Jesus is the same all the time. You never have to deal with His bad moods or grumpiness. He is always the same. That's a comfort, isn't it?

You can always know what He expects and what He wants. You can always know that He loves you ... no matter what ... and that He wants the best for you.

ChallengePoint

Sometimes Jesus is described as an anchor in life – in the way that an anchor holds a boat in place, Jesus is your anchor that holds you in place. That's something you can depend on ... always.

"Therefore, whoever humbles himself like this child is the greatest in the kingdom of heaven."

Matthew 18:4

Did you ever think you would hear God say that grown-ups should be like children? Well, here you go – this verse is proof.

Why does God say this? In seeking salvation it's important to know that you've done nothing to deserve it; you didn't earn it. An innocent child is more likely to feel that way than an adult.

ChallengePoint

Keep your childlike humility as you seek salvation and growth in your faith. You've done nothing to deserve the gifts God gives. But your humility makes you great in His eyes.

Being Thankful

Enter His gates with thanksgiving; go into His courts with praise. Give thanks to Him and bless His name.

Psalm 100:4

Why does the Bible tell you to be thankful to God? 'Cause when you take time to think about all He does for you and all He gives you, it helps you realize how much He loves you.

Then there's kind of a building effect – a little bit of thankfulness becomes a little more, then a little more. Thanksgiving grows into praise.

ChallengePoint

What are you thankful for right now? Think about it. When you come up with one thing, then think of a second and a third. You will see your thankfulness grow into praise.

Celebrating Him

And they were calling to one another: "Holy, holy, holy is the Lord Almighty; the whole earth is full of His glory."

Isaiah 6:3

Sometimes when a kid gets to meet his hero, whether it's an athlete or musician or whatever, he is so awed that he can't even speak.

Do you ever wonder what you will do when you see God? Will you be so dumbfounded that you can't utter a word? Will you fall to your knees? Or maybe like the people in this verse, you will just start celebrating Him by shouting out how awesome and holy He is!

ChallengePoint

There's no doubt that it's going to be amazing to stand in God's presence. Amazing. Whatever your response is, you will be celebrating Him and who He is! It will be a party of praise!

Knowing God by

Enduring

We also pray that you will be strengthened with all His glorious power so you will have all the endurance and patience you need. May you be filled with joy, always thanking the Father. He has enabled you to share in the inheritance that belongs to His people, who live in the light.

Colossians 1:11-12

Think of a marathon runner. His body is able to endure for the 26.3 mile race because he trains his muscles by constant running practice. He feeds his body the right nutrition it needs to be able to endure such a race.

In your Christian life you need to do the same kinds of things. Strengthen your heart and soul with God's power. That's the only way you will be able to endure whatever life brings you.

ChallengePoint

God wants you to endure and be filled with joy at the same time. There is satisfaction in finishing well. There is joy in endurance through Christ's power.

It makes a lot of sense to be a person of few words and to stay calm.

Proverbs 17:27

Why did the writer of Proverbs put these two things together: use few words and stay calm? Because a person who loses his temper usually ends up saying things he doesn't mean – things that hurt other people.

Living like Christ means not doing that. Be smart and know when to be quiet.

ChallengePoint

Keep your temper under control. Think about the words you say and how they will make other people feel. Be like Christ. Be wise.

Being Like Christ

You must be compassionate, just as your Father is compassionate.

Luke 6:36

Compassionate? That's so girly!" Okay, did you just think that? Well, you couldn't be more wrong.

Being compassionate just means caring about other people. Caring about their problems, their worries, their fears. Caring ... just as you want others to care about you.

ChallengePoint

Christ is your example. He cared about other people. He often helped them with their problems. Even if you can't actually help someone, you can pray for them. Show that you are compassionate – like Christ – by praying for others.

Being Like Christ

Serving God does make us very rich, if we are satisfied with what we have. We brought nothing into the world, so we can take nothing out.

1 Timothy 6:6-7

Some people spend all their energy and strength trying to get more "stuff." They seem to think that the guy with the most stuff wins this game of life.

Not true. If you spend all your time and energy working to get money to buy stuff that you have to take care of and actually use, but you ignore your relationship with God and even ignore other people – you lose.

ChallengePoint

Being like Christ means building a strong relationship with God and paying attention to other people. That's all that really matters. When life on this earth ends you can't take any "stuff" with you to heaven, so don't worry about it. Spend your energy on what really matters.

Knowing God by
Loving Others

"The second command is this: 'Love your neighbor as you love yourself.' There are no commands more important than these."

Mark 12:31

Jesus had just gotten through saying that the first commandment is to love God with all your heart, all your soul, all your mind, and all your strength.

He followed that up with these words. Loving others is just as important as loving God. Did you get that? It's JUST AS IMPORTANT as loving God. That's amazing.

ChallengePoint

This leaves no doubt about how God feels about how you treat other people. Love them. Get your own ego and agenda out of the way and just care for others.

Love isn't selfish or quick tempered. It doesn't keep a record of wrongs that others do.

1 Corinthians 13:5

You've heard that once God forgives your sins, He wipes them out of His memory. That's unlike a person who might hold onto memories of wrongs to throw at you the next time he gets angry with you.

God's love – true love – doesn't demand its own way. He wants you to love and serve Him because you love Him. His love isn't irritable because He's tired or moody. His love wipes away all wrongs.

ChallengePoint

God's true love forgives and forgets. That's the model, though it's not easy to do. Ask God to teach you to love others the way He loves you.

Showing Courage

The eternal God is your refuge, and His everlasting arms are under you.

Deuteronomy 33:27

Being courageous would be easy if you absolutely-without-a-doubt knew that you couldn't be hurt and couldn't lose.

Well, you CAN know that because God promises to be your refuge – the place you can hide from your enemies. He also promises to be your safety net. His strong arms are always under you to catch you when you fall.

ChallengePoint

This Scripture verse doesn't mean you won't have problems – you will. It doesn't mean you won't hurt sometimes – you will. It does mean that God is always with you and He won't let you have problems or pain so terrible that you can't recover. He will catch you.

He will destroy death forever. The LORD God will wipe away every tear from every face. He will take away the shame of His people from the earth. The LORD has spoken.

Isaiah 25:8

God is going to win. That's the bottom line. Whatever junk is going on in this world – whatever battles it seems like Satan is winning – it will all eventually end and God will win the war.

He will defeat death because His children will be able to live forever. He will win over everything done and said against His work.

ChallengePoint

Wow! God is going to win. He's going to defeat everything! And His power is on your side. He loves you so His power works for you, protects you and guides you. How awesome is that?

Abiding in Him

I ask only one thing from the LORD. This is what I want: Let me live in the LORD's house all my life. Let me see the LORD's beauty and look with my own eyes at His Temple.

Psalm 27:4

What do you think about this prayer? It's a powerful choice to ask to always be with God and be happy with obeying Him and thinking about Him.

Think about it – would you be willing to pray this? It would mean abiding with Him ... doing what He commands ... not doing what the other guys (who don't care about God) sometimes think is fun.

ChallengePoint

Asking to always be in God's presence is really kind of weird, because He has already told you that He is always with you. He knows what you're doing, thinking and saying – ALL THE TIME.

Knowing God by

His Love

This hope will never disappoint us, because God has poured out His love to fill our hearts. He gave us His love through the Holy Spirit, whom God has given to us.

Romans 5:5

Is the Holy Spirit kind of a mystery to you? Yeah, it's kind of hard to understand how God is three Persons and yet only one Person. The important thing to understand though is that God, the Holy Spirit, lives in your heart.

He's that little urge you feel to do the right thing sometimes. He's the voice in your mind that warns you about a bad choice. God gave the Holy Spirit to live in your heart because He loves you. The Holy Spirit is His presence with you always.

ChallengePoint

The Holy Spirit came to earth when Jesus went back to heaven. He is God's presence – His gift of love to His children. Pay attention to His guidance and direction in your heart.

Knowing God by

His Love

October 24

"For God loved the world so much that He gave His one and only Son, so that everyone who believes in Him will not perish but have eternal life."

John 3:16

It can't be any more obvious than this. God gave His own Son – His only Son – because He loves you. He sent Jesus to earth, knowing that He was not going to be treated well. It was going to be tough for Him. People would treat Him badly and then kill Him.

It is because of Jesus' death and then His resurrection (His victory over death) that you can have a real relationship with God!

ChallengePoint

That's how much God loves you. His love cost Him something. He probably could have come up with another plan for you to be able to go to heaven. But this one cost Him something, so it shows you how much He loves you.

Praying

Depend on the LORD; trust Him, and He will take care of you. Then your goodness will shine like the sun, and your fairness like the noonday sun.

Psalm 37:5-6

Be reasonable ... how can you expect God to help you if you don't talk to Him? Tell Him what you're facing, whether it's a difficult test, a big game, a concert, a problem with a friend or trouble in your family.

Commit it to Him – trust Him to take care of it and to help you through it.

ChallengePoint

This doesn't mean God will instantly wipe away your problem or difficulty. It means He will be with you and strengthen you to get through it. You will be in a better place because you trusted Him.

Seeking His Protection

*Surely Your goodness and unfailing love will pursue me all the days of my life, and I will live in the house of the L*ORD *forever.*

Psalm 23:6

This Scripture verse seems kind of like a shepherd's job description. A shepherd moves around behind his flock and guides them into safety.

God's love is pursuing you – moving around behind you and guiding you into safety with Him. He loves you and wants to protect you.

ChallengePoint

All of God's children need to be shepherded. Some think they know what's best for them, but they really don't. Let God guide, direct and shepherd you into safety through His love.

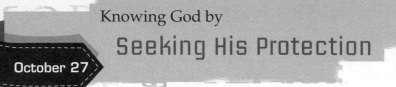

Knowing God by
Seeking His Protection

"Don't be afraid. I am with you. Don't tremble with fear. I am your God. I will make you strong, as I protect you with My arm and give you victories."

Isaiah 41:10

Sometimes the scariest thing is being alone. If you're in an unfamiliar place you don't know which way to go. You don't know how to find your way out and you don't know if the place where you find yourself in is dangerous.

You can trust God to always be with you – you're never alone. He says you don't have to be afraid because He is always with you.

ChallengePoint

Take courage in God's presence with you. If you become frightened and a little discouraged, stop and remind yourself that God is with you and will always, always help you.

Put all evil things out of your life: sexual sinning, doing evil, letting evil thoughts control you, wanting things that are evil, and greed. This is really serving a false god.

Colossians 3:5

You can hide things from others (yeah, even your parents) but you cannot hide them from God.

The places you visit on the Internet – He sees. The movies and TV shows you watch – He knows about. The jokes you and your buddies tell – He hears. Are you embarrassed to know what He knows about you?

ChallengePoint

Don't get caught up in the junk of this world and think it's more important than God. It isn't. Nothing is more important than serving and honoring Him, even though it makes you "different" from the other guys sometimes. It's worth it.

Obeying Him

Choose today whom you will serve ... but as for me and my family, we will serve the LORD.

Joshua 24:15

Take a stand. Show some backbone. Be brave. Those are some phrases that come to mind with this verse.

Decide if you're going to obey God. Decide ... because if you don't decide you are deciding you aren't. Get it? Not to decide is to decide. There's no middle of the road here. Choose to obey God.

ChallengePoint

Yep, no middle of the road. Don't think you're going to wait to decide for God when you're older – do that and you're making a choice right now. Choose today (and every day) to serve God.

Knowing God by
Obeying Him

But, LORD, we are waiting for Your way of justice. Our souls want to remember You and Your name.

Isaiah 26:8

Here's the bottom line: If you aren't obeying God, then you aren't trusting Him. If you aren't trusting Him, then you aren't glorifying Him.

Obeying is the foundation for all the other things to be built on.

ChallengePoint

What does God really mean to your life? You can say you love Him and trust Him, but if you aren't obeying Him ... then all those words are just lies.

Being Faithful

God will bless you, if you don't give up when your faith is being tested. He will reward you with a glorious life, just as He rewards everyone who loves Him.

James 1:12

How do your muscles get stronger? By working them hard, right? When you exercise and work your muscles they get stronger and work longer and harder.

Your faith is like that too. It's through the hard times that it grows. During problems is when you learn that God will take care of you and that He will help and strengthen you.

ChallengePoint

Faith doesn't really grow in easy times, because you don't need to see then that God is protecting you, guiding you and loving you. In the problems that life brings, you see that God is with you and taking care of you. Your faith grows a little stronger each time you see that.

You are uniquely God's –
a one-of-a-kind design!
– Anonymous

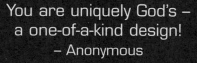

November

Seeking Salvation

He saved us, not because of the righteous things we had done, but because of His mercy. He washed away our sins, giving us a new birth and new life through the Holy Spirit.

Titus 3:5

What are you saved from?

1. Your sins – the nasty, mean, evil and selfish things you think, say and do.
2. Hell – separation from God forever and ever.

What are you saved for?

1. A friendship and relationship with God.
2. Heaven – being with God forever.

ChallengePoint

Have you made the choice for salvation? Salvation is as simple as asking Jesus to be your Savior, forgive your sin, and live in your heart.

Knowing God by
Being Thankful

Give thanks to the LORD and pray to Him. Tell the nations what He has done.

1 Chronicles 16:8

When you make an effort to do something to help someone – something that isn't expected or required – it's nice to be thanked, isn't it?

God appreciates being thanked for what He does, but not just because He wants thanks. He wants you to think about how much He loves you. Thinking about what to thank Him for makes you think about all He does.

ChallengePoint

Take time to thank God for all He does for you. Tell others about His love, His kindness and His gifts.

Make a joyful symphony before the LORD! Let the sea and everything in it shout their songs of joy before the LORD.

Psalm 98:6-9

Creation shouts God's praise all the time. Think about it ... when the ocean waves crash to the shore they are saying, "Praise God who created this!"

When a tiny flower pushes up through the soil, it's praising God. When the wind ripples through the high branches of a tree, it's celebrating God. Creation praises Him every day.

ChallengePoint

Is it kind of weird to think that the things you expect to happen in nature are really songs of praise to God? OK, but what or who makes those "normal" things happen? God does. So nature sings back its praise to Him. Do you do the same?

Being Like Christ

"Where your treasure is, there your heart will be also."

Matthew 6:21

Answer this question: What is the most important thing in your life? Got an answer? Good. Now, answer this question: On what do you spend most of your thoughts time and energy? Do the two answers match in any way?

Whatever you spend most of your thoughts and energy on is REALLY what's most important to you.

ChallengePoint

Is living for Christ important to you? If it is, then your thoughts, prayers, time and energy will be directed toward doing that. If it isn't, then you will not spend much time on it.

Loving Others

We don't need to write to you about the importance of loving each other, for God Himself has taught you to love one another.

1 Thessalonians 4:9

When you get a lesson from God, you'd better pay attention. God says over and over that it's important to Him that people love one another. It's not good enough to just love your family and friends. It's not even good enough to love people who are a lot like you.

God says to love your enemies and those who think and live differently than you do.

ChallengePoint

It's easier to ignore people who are different from you. It's easiest to say mean things about your enemies. The easy thing is not to love them. It's the hard thing to love them. It's the right thing to do, though.

Giving

God can bless you with everything you need, and you will always have more than enough to do all kinds of good things for others.

2 Corinthians 9:8

God gives you stuff so you can share with others. If you have two of something, give one to someone who has none.

Get it? God does not give stuff to you to make you wealthy. He gives so you can help those who do not have enough to live.

ChallengePoint

The world is filled with people who don't have a home, enough food, shoes, backpacks for their kids, medicine … and on and on. God says it is the responsibility of those who have plenty to help those who do not have enough.

Suppressing Our Pride

This is the reason: God lives forever and is holy. He is high and lifted up. He says, "I live in a high and holy place, but I also live with people who are sad and humble. I give new life to those who are humble and to those whose hearts are broken."

Isaiah 57:15

Look who lives in heaven with God ... those who are humble. Pride gets you nowhere in God's eyes.

A person who is humble is more likely to be repentant of his sins and willing to submit to God. It makes him more loving and encouraging to others too. That makes a person more appealing to God.

ChallengePoint

God puts so much importance on the command to love others. It's not really possible to be filled with pride in yourself, bragging about yourself, and also be encouraging and supportive to others. God is much more pleased with humility – it allows you to be others-focused.

Knowing God by
Trusting Him

You love Him even though you have never seen Him. Though you do not see Him now, you trust Him; and you rejoice with a glorious, inexpressible joy.

1 Peter 1:8

People who get excited about a politician running for office listen to his speeches, and read articles about him and what he will do once elected. They cheer for him at his meetings, put his bumper stickers on their cars, wear buttons promoting him and finally ... vote for him. They really get behind their guy.

Think how different that is from trusting God. You can't really SEE God. You can't HEAR His campaign speeches or go to His rallies. Much of being on God's team has to be taken by faith. You trust Him because of what you read about Him in the Bible and what others teach you about Him.

ChallengePoint

Trust of God is founded on faith — believing in what you cannot actually see. The reward for that is glorious, in-expressible joy!

Using His Gifts

"Here I am! I stand at the door and knock. If you hear My voice and open the door, I will come in and eat with you, and you will eat with Me."

Revelation 3:20

Imagine sitting down with the most famous, skilled athlete in the world – maybe a top Olympic athlete. That would be quite an honor, wouldn't it? Would you be a little shy and tongue-tied or would you have a zillion questions for him?

What does this have to do with using God's gifts? Hey ... Jesus, the Creator of everything there is, will sit down and have dinner with you and talk with you as a friend. How cool is that?

ChallengePoint

What a gift – Jesus will share a meal with you. Even more amazing is that Jesus knocks at the door of your heart and waits for you to open it. He doesn't come barreling in like a bull in a china shop. He waits for you to invite Him in.

When the kindness and love of God our Savior appeared, He saved us, not because of righteous things we had done, but because of His mercy. He saved us through the washing of rebirth and renewal by the Holy Spirit.

Titus 3:4-5

Actions speak louder than words. You've probably heard that statement before and the fact is – it's really true. You can say whatever you think you're supposed to say but if your actions don't back up what you say, people will pay more attention to your actions and will think your words are lies.

God doesn't just talk about loving you, His actions back up His words. He saves you from your sins – love can't get any more active than that.

ChallengePoint

God's actions wash away your sins and give you new life through the Holy Spirit – also a gift from Him. Words of love backed up by actions of love. Good example, eh?

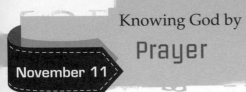

Knowing God by

Prayer

This is the boldness we have in God's presence: that if we ask God for anything that agrees with what He wants, He hears us.

1 John 5:14

When your mom is trying to get you to clean up your room, does she have to ask you over and over again? Do you not really listen to her until her voice reaches a certain decibel level? It's kind of like that when you know she is really serious, right? Now, if she asks you to do something you want to do, it's a whole different story. You hear her on the first word, don't you?

When you ask God for help, He hears you on the first try. He promises that. The only key is that He hears when you ask for things that please Him. What's that all about? Well, if you ask Him to make an enemy crash and burn – He probably won't pay much attention – if you ask for things that show love for Him and others, He will hear right away.

ChallengePoint

God wants to hear your prayers. He wants to answer them too. The prayers of a guy who is trying to obey God and live for Him will please God.

Then you will experience God's peace, which exceeds anything we can understand. His peace will guard your hearts and minds as you live in Christ Jesus.

Philippians 4:7

Have you ever been to a party where there was a piñata filled with candy? Blindfolded kids take turns banging sticks against the piñata until it finally pops open and candy rains out for everyone.

That image of a stick repeatedly hitting the piñata until it's broken is what this verse of protection brings up.

Satan's darts of worry, fear, self-centeredness and low self-esteem bang against your heart day after day. God's peace is the protection that cushions your heart so it is not broken by Satan's darts.

ChallengePoint

God's peace protects your heart and mind. You need that protection from Him to live in peace and obedience to Him. His peace is what tells you that Satan's darts are lies. All of them.

Serving Him

Then Jesus said to His followers, "If people want to follow Me, they must give up the things they want. They must be willing even to give up their lives to follow Me."

Matthew 16:24

The message of this Scripture verse is "Get yourself out of the way." Plain and simple. You can't serve God and keep your own agenda going of what you want to do and what you want to accomplish.

Know why? IT ISN'T ABOUT YOU. Forget your plans. Do what God wants you to do – even the stuff that isn't so much fun. Just follow Him.

ChallengePoint

Some of the stuff God wants you to do may be stuff you don't enjoy. It may be background stuff that pushes someone else to star status. It may be dirty work. So what? It's what God wants you to do and serving God is about Him, not about you.

So you have not received a spirit that makes you fearful slaves. Instead, you received God's Spirit when He adopted you as His own children. Now we call Him, "Abba, Father."

Romans 8:15

Slaves do what they are told to do. They do not think for themselves. Their obedience is based on fear.

Obeying God is not that way. God adopted you as His son. He's your Father. Hopefully you know that means you don't need to fear Him. You can obey Him because you love Him and He loves you.

ChallengePoint

It may be hard to imagine what a slave's life is like. Hopefully you will never have to know. As God's child you have His Holy Spirit living in you. You are His child. The desire to obey Him should come from love for Him then.

Keep your lives free from the love of money, and be satisfied with what you have. God has said, "I will never leave you; I will never abandon you."

Hebrews 13:5

Money! Money! Money! Get more money! Make more money! It's all about MONEY!

That's the message that TV, movies, Internet and magazines would have you believe. Most of the world thinks that success is only indicated by how much money you make.

God says that's not true. God says to be satisfied with what you have – your wealth comes from the fact that God will always help you. He will always be with you.

ChallengePoint

When Jesus lived on earth, He didn't even have a home. He depended on others for a place to sleep and for food to eat. He was satisfied with that. It goes against everything the world teaches, but the truth is that real wealth comes from having God in your life.

Knowing God by
His Forgiveness

Since God chose you to be the holy people He loves, you must clothe yourselves with tenderhearted mercy, kindness, humility, gentleness, and patience. Make allowance for each other's faults, and forgive anyone who offends you. Remember, the Lord forgave you, so you must forgive others.

Colossians 3:12-13

OK, since God forgives you over and over and over ... you should be willing to forgive others. The message here is, "Don't accept something that you aren't willing to pass along to others."

You are a member of God's family and that means you are to exhibit the same qualities He has – kindness, gentleness, patience and forgiveness.

ChallengePoint

Let people see the family likeness. Others should be able to see God in how you live and act. The understanding that you are forgiven should make you forgiving.

Understanding Anger

"I promise you that if you are angry with someone, you will have to stand trial. If you call someone a fool, you will be taken to court. And if you say that someone is worthless, you will be in danger of the fires of hell."

Matthew 5:22

Whoa! God is SERIOUS about anger. You'd better keep yours under control. Look at this:

1. Get angry – you're going to be judged for it.
2. Call someone names – you could be taken to court.
3. Curse someone – you're in danger of the fires of hell.

ChallengePoint

Pay attention. When you get mad at someone, STOP! Ask God to help you keep your emotions under control! It's important to do that!

Seeking Salvation

Put on your new nature, created to be like God – truly righteous and holy.

Ephesians 4:24

Have you ever been outside playing with your friends when it started to rain? By the time you got all your toys gathered up and ran home, you were soaked and probably muddy. Your mom might have made you take off your shoes outside so you didn't track mud in. You were, to put it simply, dirty.

Well, face it dude, before God saves you, your insides are dirty too. They are stained by sin. When God saves you, you get a clean, new nature. You get to sort of start over – and be like God – righteous and holy.

ChallengePoint

God cleans up your dirty heart. He gives you a clean new heart that wants to serve Him and obey Him. This isn't a new physical heart that pumps blood in your body – it's the heart in your spirit and soul that wants to serve Him. He makes you clean and new!

Knowing God by

Being Thankful

November 19

He threw himself at Jesus' feet and thanked Him – and he was a Samaritan.

Luke 17:16

When was the last time you fell down at someone's feet and thanked them for something? Yeah, probably NEVER. Here's the rest of this story though: Jesus healed ten men of a terrible disease. They had a disease so bad that they couldn't live in town near other people. They even had to leave their families.

Jesus healed the ten men. All ten men ran toward town without even saying, "Hey, thanks." Only one man came back when he remembered to thank Jesus. This one man was a Samaritan – an enemy of Jesus' people. Weird, huh?

ChallengePoint

A man, who in any other circumstance would have been Jesus' enemy, fell at His feet and thanked Him for His healing power. Nine men who were of the same nationality and faith as Jesus did not say thanks. Learn from this Samaritan man … thank Jesus for all He does for you.

At the name of Jesus everyone will bow down, those in heaven, on earth, and under the earth.

Philippians 2:10

A celebration doesn't have to mean whooping and shouting and high-fiving your buddies. Some celebrations are quiet and awestruck. You can celebrate God by dropping to your knees in worship. One day every person will do that and every person will confess that Jesus is Lord.

For some people it will be too late – they will be recognizing Jesus from their condemned place of hell. You can celebrate Him now in whatever way you choose.

ChallengePoint

Celebrate Him. Worship Him. Tell others about Him. Bow your knees before Him and confess Him with your voice.

Being Like Christ

You are not controlled by your sinful nature. You are controlled by the Spirit if you have the Spirit of God living in you. (And remember that those who do not have the Spirit of Christ living in them do not belong to Him at all.)

Romans 8:9

Who controls the TV remote at your house? Family wars have broken out over remote controls. Of course, whoever has it controls what program is playing on the screen. There's a lot of power behind the hand that holds the remote.

Control is the issue – who controls you? If the Holy Spirit is living in you because you've asked Christ into your heart, then He should be the One in control of you ... not your old sinful nature.

ChallengePoint

The problem is that your old sinful nature never really goes away. It keeps trying to get the remote control to your heart back in its hands. It's a constant battle and one that you help the Holy Spirit win by daily giving your life to Him. Make the choice to put the control in His hands.

Being Like Christ

We all make many mistakes. If people never said anything wrong, they would be perfect and able to control their entire selves, too.

James 3:2

Wouldn't you sometimes like to just wrap duct tape around your mouth? That may seem like the best way to keep it shut! Controlling what you say and how you say it is really hard! And, unfortunately, the words you say often hurt other people and even damage your reputation as a Christ-follower.

Of course, if you could control your words then you could control your thoughts and actions too. The bottom line is, that is not going to happen, so you'd better ask God for His help.

ChallengePoint

Realistically speaking you can't live your life with duct tape wrapped around your mouth. It would look funny and make it difficult to eat and drink. So ... use God's duct tape ... His Holy Spirit. Ask Him to help you control your words and your thoughts and actions. Ask Him to help you live like Christ.

Knowing God by

Loving Others

Jesus answered, "The most important command is this: 'Listen, people of Israel! The Lord our God is the only Lord. Love the Lord your God with all your heart, all your soul, all your mind, and all your strength.' The second command is this: 'Love your neighbor as you love yourself.' There are no commands more important than these."

Mark 12:29-31

These Scripture verses and others like it appear in several places in the Bible. Why does it keep showing up? Because it's important. God insists on your complete devotion, heart, soul, mind and strength.

There are some things in life that you can get away with giving half your attention to ... loving God is not one of them.

ChallengePoint

The term "sitting on the fence" comes to mind here – not being willing to fully commit to either loving God or not loving God. Don't ride the fence on this. Give God everything. You'll never be sorry.

Showing Love

Most important of all, continue to show deep love for each other, for love covers a multitude of sins.

1 Peter 4:8

You live with other people. You go to school with other people. You are on teams with people ... the point is that you're around people all the time.

There are going to be times when you don't get things right – times when you mess up and do dumb things. It's OK. Real love can cover over those times. People will forgive you for your bad behavior if they know that you really do love them.

ChallengePoint

Love is so important in relating to others. It's important because God says it's important. You know that if someone says something mean to you but you know that deep down inside they really love you, then you're much more likely to forgive them. Let your love for others show.

Refuse to give in to him, by standing strong in your faith. You know that your Christian family all over the world is having the same kinds of suffering. And after you suffer for a short time, God, who gives all grace, will make everything right. He will make you strong and support you and keep you from falling. He called you to share in His glory in Christ, a glory that will continue forever. All power is His forever and ever.

1 Peter 5:9-11

Life is stinky sometimes. There's no way around that. Bad things happen, even to good people. When the bad things come, do you wonder where God is? Do you wonder why He doesn't just fix things for you?

That question has been asked a million times through the years by lots of people. There is no easy answer. But one reason is that it is when things get tough and you need help that you see God's power. You experience Him helping you, lifting you up and strengthening you.

ChallengePoint

Hard times are necessary in order to appreciate good times. The stress of problems makes your faith grow stronger. Trust God enough to endure the tough times.

Knowing God by
Using His Gifts

"Teach these new disciples to obey all the commands I have given you. And be sure of this: I am with you always, even to the end of the age."

Matthew 28:20

Two gifts from God are outlined here:

1. People who will teach you about God's commands.
2. God will always be with you – forever.

Pretty cool how God instructs people to help each other learn about Him. Then He encourages you to keep on doing His work with His strength and presence, which will always be with you.

ChallengePoint

Make use of God's gifts – people around you who can help you learn about Him. Then pass that along to others who you can teach. You never have to do this alone – God is always with you!

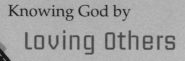

Knowing God by
Loving Others

We love because God loved us first.

1 John 4:19

When you want to learn a new skill – whether it's in sports, music or on a video game – the easiest way to learn it is from someone who has already mastered it. Learn from the master, right? Well, you can sure do that when it comes to learning how to love.

God loved you first – before time began; in fact, before YOU began. He loves you no matter what. So He can sure teach you a lot about love.

ChallengePoint

You loving others is important to God – it's a command. God loved you first. As you experience God's love, which is completely undeserved, you should be more willing to love others. If you can't or don't know how, let God teach you.

Your commands make me wiser than my enemies, because they are mine forever.

Psalm 119:98

Secret weapons! Ha ha! Secret weapons are what help you defeat the evil enemy. Your secret weapon is God's Word. His commands guide you.

His Word shows you what is right and wrong. His Word should be your constant guide. It is your advantage in this life – it makes you smarter than your enemies.

ChallengePoint

God's Word is only your secret weapon if you use it. So spend time each day reading His Word. Look for His guidance from its words. Look for instructions as to how to live for Him.

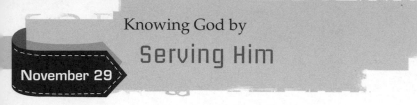

Knowing God by

Serving Him

November 29

Do not be fooled: You cannot cheat God. People harvest only what they plant.

Galatians 6:7

If you wanted a big crop of corn on the cob, you wouldn't plant green beans, would you? Whatever seeds you plant is what will grow. That's just common sense.

How does that bit of gardening news relate to serving God? Like this: What you put into serving God is what you get out of it. So, if you serve half-heartedly, don't expect major joy and blessings.

ChallengePoint

Harvesting what you plant is fair and honest. It puts the responsibility on you to make a choice as to how you will live your life. Are you going to give God everything? If you're not, then don't expect Him to give you everything.

Obeying Him

The Lord leads with unfailing love and faithfulness all who keep His covenant and obey His demands.

Psalm 25:10

Training for a competition in a sport is a lot of work. You work and work for several hours a day for months, maybe even years. The reward is when you step onto the playing field or the court and know that you are ready to play – trained to the best of your ability.

Obeying God has rewards too. It's not always easy and it is a learning process, but the reward is God's love and faithfulness to you. What could be better than that?

ChallengePoint

Having God lead you and knowing that His love is constant is worth the effort of obeying God. You do not have to learn to obey by yourself, God will help you. His Word will teach and guide you.

You are valuable because
you exist. Not because of what
you do or what you have done,
but simply because you are.
– Max Lucado

December

Serving Him

You yourself must be an example to them by doing good works of every kind. Let everything you do reflect the integrity and seriousness of your teaching.

Titus 2:7

Do you know what an ambassador is? It's a person who travels to other countries representing his own country. The things this ambassador does, gives others an idea of what his country believes and what's important to his government.

You are an ambassador – of God. That means you need to be careful how you live, what you say and how you represent God.

ChallengePoint

Okay, you're just a kid, but even at your age everything you do reflects what you really feel about God. It takes an effort to think about how you live, what you say and how you represent God. But it's important.

"If you obey My commands, you will remain in My love, just as I have obeyed My Father's commands and remain in His love."

John 15:10

Jesus gave you an example to follow. Hey, if obeying was good enough for Jesus, why should you fight it, right?

Jesus' example of obedience was constant and steady. When you obey God your relationship with Him stays healthy. Your communication with Him, your experience of His love ... all is well.

ChallengePoint

Obeying God's commandments keeps your relationship with Him healthy. So you never need to doubt His love for you. Jesus is your model.

His Forgiveness

You were cleansed; you were made holy; you were made right with God by calling on the name of the Lord Jesus Christ and by the Spirit of our God.

1 Corinthians 6:11

Some things are hard to learn. Some are not. Some are complicated. Some are not. Some have many steps to achieve. Some do not. Some things are made more complicated than they need to be.

God's forgiveness is not complicated. When you ask Jesus into your heart, God forgives your sin. You are cleansed.

ChallengePoint

It's so simple because that's the way God wanted it to be. He wanted salvation to be available to anyone who wanted it, because He loves all people. God's forgiveness cleans your heart and makes you set apart for God's work.

Seeking His Guidance

God always does what He plans, and that's why He appointed Christ to choose us.

Ephesians 1:11

Video games have a plan. You do this or that and you move to the next level. You continue moving up the levels to win the game.

God has a plan for you. Yep, and He came up with it before you were even born and decided to follow Him. From the minute you entered this earth He started working out His plan in your life.

ChallengePoint

God's plan is for you to become the best person possible. He will guide you in obeying Him, serving Him, and loving Him.

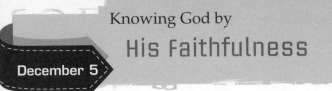

Knowing God by

His Faithfulness

"However, those the Father has given Me will come to Me, and I will never reject them."

John 6:37

What can you absolutely count on in this world? That the sun will always come up in the morning and set at night? Yes, except when it didn't (it happened once in the Old Testament). That the oceans will stay put where they're supposed to be? Yes, except when it didn't (remember the Red Sea?).

The one thing you can absolutely count on is God. When you come to the Father, you become His and He will always, always be with you.

ChallengePoint

When God says something, He means it. You can count on it forever, no matter what. God says that once you are His, He will never reject you. You are His.

Seeking His Protection

The Lord is faithful, and He will strengthen and protect you from the evil one.

2 Thessalonians 3:3

Just in case you have any doubts, there is an evil presence in this world – the devil. You can't blame everything on him, but some of the rotten things in this world are certainly because of him.

Just in case you have any doubts, God will stand guard over you. He will protect you from the Evil One.

ChallengePoint

Stay close to God. He will take care of you. There is an evil presence in the world that is constantly trying to trip you up and make you fall away from God. Only God can protect you.

Let the words of Christ, in all their richness live in your hearts and make you wise. Use His words to teach and counsel each other. Sing psalms and hymns and spiritual songs to God with thankful hearts.

Colossians 3:16

Garbage in ... garbage out. The food you put in your body determines whether your body is healthy or overweight and sickly. The information put into a computer determines the things the computer can do.

At some level, what is put into something determines what comes out. Put the words of Christ in your heart and that will bring good stuff out of your heart.

ChallengePoint

Good stuff that comes from Christ's words going into your heart includes wisdom and thankfulness. Only good things come from the words of Christ in your life. His words give you a lot to be thankful for.

Celebrating Him

December 8

This will happen on that day when the Lord returns to be praised and honored by all who have faith in Him and belong to Him. This includes you, because you believed what we said.

2 Thessalonians 1:10

You've seen the celebrations when a professional sports team wins a big championship. Their city throws a major parade, often called a ticker tape parade. Strips of paper are thrown from tall buildings onto the champions. People line the streets cheering for them. Quite a celebration!

Well, there's going to be a celebration like that for Jesus when He comes back. Everyone on earth will recognize Him as the Lord – the Son of God. It will be the most awesome celebration ever!

ChallengePoint

The day will come when the whole earth recognizes God's power and His place as Creator and Savior. The celebration will be like nothing you've ever experienced. Don't you want to be a part of it?

Being Like Christ

"You will know the truth, and the truth will set you free."

John 8:32

Do you memorize Bible verses? Do you memorize them for things other than club program awards or quiz contests? Why should you? Because those verses are the key to surviving problems and even growing.

Jesus quoted Scripture back to Satan when He was being tempted. If it's important for Jesus to know Scripture, then it must be important for you too.

ChallengePoint

Jesus often quoted Scripture. That means He must have read the Old Testament and committed it to memory. The verses of the Bible are the weapons you need to fight against Satan's attacks.

You are joined together with peace through the Spirit, so make every effort to continue together in this way.

Ephesians 4:3

The five athletes who work together as a basketball team must be united. They must know the plays, anticipate one another's moves and have the same goal of winning.

Being united with your team-mates is absolutely necessary. It's really important for Christians to be united in the Holy Spirit. That unity keeps you at peace with others.

ChallengePoint

God's children need to live at peace with one another. Other people are watching to see how you behave. They notice whether or not you get along with each other and love each other.

Being Like Christ

Do everything without complaining and arguing, so that no one can criticize you. Live clean, innocent lives as children of God, shining like bright lights in a world full of crooked and perverse people.

Philippians 2:14-15

They are watching you. Who is watching, you ask? Everyone. Everyone who knows that you claim to be a Christ-follower. Yep, so every time you complain about something or argue with someone, they notice.

Your job in living like Christ is to be a good representative of Him. Shine brightly – look different to people who don't know Him.

ChallengePoint

Christ is trusting you to live a life that shows what He is like. Get along with other people. Don't be selfish or self-centered. Consistently live a life that shows what Christ is like.

Showing Love

Anyone who claims to be in the light but hates his brother is still in the darkness.

1 John 2:9

Have you ever played one of those games where you make a statement and the other players have to figure out if you're telling the truth or bluffing? Fun game – not so fun in real life.

You can claim to be a God-follower and maybe convince people around you that you aren't bluffing. But you won't convince God that it's the truth if you don't back up your words with loving people around you.

ChallengePoint

Loving others is a family likeness ... if you're really a part of God's family.

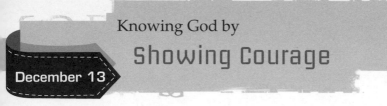

Knowing God by

Showing Courage

Obey the LORD with great fear. Be happy, but tremble.

Psalm 2:11

Think about climbing to the top of a super high rock cliff, walking out to the edge of it, gazing down at the ocean below, then doing a beautiful swan dive off the cliff. Sound like fun? Or, would you be scared silly to jump off a high cliff?

Doing something even when you're afraid is really courageous. Serving God, even when you're scared, is an awesome thing to do.

ChallengePoint

When you go ahead and do what God wants, even though it's scary to you, it shows you trust Him to take care of you and keep on guiding you.

"Heal the sick, raise the dead to life again, heal those who have skin diseases, and force demons out of people. I give you these powers freely, so help other people freely."

Matthew 10:8

OK, sign up – which of the things listed in this verse can you do? Um, maybe none of them? Then what's the deal with this verse?

Maybe you can't raise the dead or cast out demons, but you can give. God wants you to give and give and give out of whatever He has given you. Maybe all you can give is time or prayers. That's OK.

ChallengePoint

It's really important to give to others because it ties you together. It makes you a part of the same family. Helping others is the best feeling in the world. Give as often as you can in any way you can.

Knowing God by

Seeking His Protection

December 15

"*Take My yoke upon you. Let Me teach you, because I am humble and gentle at heart, and you will find rest for your souls.*"

Matthew 11:29

What's a yoke? This Scripture verse is not talking about the yellow part of the egg (that's a *yolk*).

The simple explanation of this verse is that Jesus is encouraging you to identify with Him – join His team – line up with Him. He will teach you about living for Him and He will do it with gentleness and humility.

ChallengePoint

Join Jesus' family and you can take a deep breath and relax. You can rest because He will take care of you, protect you and teach you.

Obeying Him

The Spirit produces the fruit of love, joy, peace, patience, kindness, goodness, faithfulness, gentleness, self-control. There is no law that says these things are wrong.

Galatians 5:22-23

Band practice. Say you play the clarinet. Your section (all the clarinets) practice alone. Then the whole band practices together ... for several hours ... every day. It takes a lot of work to get everyone in the band to play together and sound good. A good band director knows how to work with the members to draw the best sound for their instrument.

The Holy Spirit is like that too. He works in your heart to pull out the best characteristics from you – the ones that are like Him.

ChallengePoint

The Holy Spirit put those things in your heart. He planted them there and He will help you learn how to let it shine out in your life.

Obeying Him

"This is the new covenant I will make with the people of Israel on that day," says the Lord: "I will put My laws in their minds, and I will write them on their hearts. I will be their God, and they will be My people."

Hebrews 8:10

When you have a really big job in front of you it is nice to know that you aren't alone. You don't have to figure things out by yourself and you don't have to do the work alone.

God has promised that if you choose to obey Him, He will give you all the help you need. He loves you and wants you to be successful in obeying Him, so He will help you know His laws by putting them in your heart.

ChallengePoint

Obeying God is not always easy, because Satan will do everything he can to stop you. Temptation and confusion are a couple of his specialties. But God will help you to remember His laws because He wants you to succeed. You're not in this alone. Cool, huh?

Seeking His Guidance

David shepherded them with integrity of heart; with skillful hands he led them.

Psalm 78:72

A fishing trip into the wilderness is a lot of fun. But finding your way through the forests to the lake, and knowing where the best spot to catch fish is, can be confusing. That's where a guide comes in handy. A guide knows where he's going. He's been there before.

David was called "a man after God's own heart." He sought God's wisdom and guidance and then passed it along to others. God wants to be your guide. He's already been where you are going – deeper into a life of obedience and living for Him.

ChallengePoint

Why does God want to be your guide? Because He loves you. He cares about you so He will be your guide.

Being Obedient

"I correct and discipline everyone I love. So be diligent and turn from your indifference."

Revelation 3:19

Some guys try their best to avoid discipline. They bargain with their parents and try to cut deals to avoid punishment. It doesn't usually work though. Why do your parents discipline you? Because they love you. They know that disciplining you when you have disobeyed is the best way to help you learn to obey the next time.

As your Father, God disciplines you too. He has to because that's how you will learn from your disobedience. Don't be discouraged when God disciplines you. You can be glad that He cares enough to do that. Learn from it and try harder to be obedient the next time.

ChallengePoint

If you keep doing the same silly thing over and over – disobeying in exactly the same way – it's frustrating to your parents and probably to God too. Learn from your mistakes. Learn from your discipline and become more and more obedient.

The LORD will not abandon His chosen people.

1 Samuel 12:22

When the going gets tough, the tough ... run away." Ha! That is NOT the way the saying goes and it is NOT what God promises to do when you have hard times in your life.

God will never run away from you. He will not get tired of your problems and He will never be overwhelmed by your problems.

ChallengePoint

It's so cool to know that you are never alone. You will never get in the middle of a problem, look around and find that you're alone. God promises to be with you, help you and guide you.

Being Thankful

Thank God for His gift that is too wonderful for words!
2 Corinthians 9:15

Does your mom make you write thank-you notes for birthday or Christmas gifts? Good for her if she does. It's kind of hard, though, to be thankful for gifts like ... socks. Stuff that you may need but not really want.

God gave you an amazing gift – too wonderful for words. He thought of a gift that you not only NEED but that you would WANT – Jesus.

ChallengePoint

God's wonderful gift changes everything about your life. Jesus makes salvation and forever being with God possible. He makes living everyday life better and your relationships with others better. Good gift, huh?

Knowing God by

Suppressing Our Pride

It is not that we think we can do anything of lasting value by ourselves. Our only power and success comes from God.

2 Corinthians 3:5

Tooting your own horn gets you nowhere. Seriously, bragging about yourself and your accomplishments would be like a tree bragging about growing leaves.

Who made those leaves grow? God. Who put the branches on the tree? God. Who grew the tree itself? God. Get it?

ChallengePoint

Anything you can do. All things you are. All of it comes from God. Your skills, abilities, talents and intelligence all come from God. You can claim no credit for it. However, you can ... and should ... thank Him every day!

Serving Him

You, my son Solomon, accept the God of your father. Serve Him completely and willingly, because the LORD knows what is in everyone's mind. He understands everything you think. If you go to Him for help, you will get an answer. But if you turn away from Him, He will leave you forever.

1 Chronicles 28:9

The first time a chess board is plopped down in front of you and all the pieces are set up, do you think you could just start playing – and even win? Not likely, especially if you're playing someone who really knows the game. You have to know the rules of the game. You need to study some of the moves and know the strategy.

The same is true of serving God. It helps to get to know Him and to know His Word, which is chock-full of instructions. You can try just faking your devotion to Him, but, um, He sees your heart so He'd know you don't mean it.

ChallengePoint

If you want to serve God, give it all you have. Get to know Him. Talk with Him. Read His Word. Make sure your heart is devoted to Him, because that's what He is going to look at – not all you are doing – but WHY you are doing it.

Abiding in Him

"When you cross deep rivers, I will be with you, and you won't drown. When you walk through fire, you won't be burned or scorched by the flames."

Isaiah 43:2

Insulation is wonderful stuff. It's put between the walls and above the ceilings when houses are built. It keeps heat inside in the winter and heat outside in the summer. It makes living in the house more comfortable.

Unfortunately, your life can't be insulated against trouble. Life just gets stinky sometimes and you have to deal with it. BUT you don't have to deal with it alone. God promises to stick close to you. He promises to be with you in all those stinky times. You'll never be alone.

ChallengePoint

It's nice to know that you don't have to face the hard times alone, isn't it? God is with you, and that means He is strengthening you, helping you, guiding you. You don't have to plough through problems by yourself.

His Love

"Even to your old age and gray hairs I am He, I am He who will sustain you. I have made you and I will carry you; I will sustain you and I will rescue you."

Isaiah 46:4

Blood is thicker than water. That's what people say when they are explaining how family members stick up for each other. Family members are loyal to one another and stand together against others.

That's true of God's family too. Blood is thicker than water, and it is Jesus' blood that makes you a member of God's family. Then He sticks close to you – for your whole life!

ChallengePoint

God's love is what sent Jesus to earth on that first Christmas long ago. It was the beginning of His plan to make a way for you to be able to know Him. He promises to take care of you for your whole life. Love holds you close and you're never alone!

Seeking His Protection

God is strong and can help you not to fall. He can bring you before His glory without any wrong in you and can give you great joy. He is the only God, the One who saves us. To Him be glory, greatness, power, and authority through Jesus Christ our Lord for all time past, now, and forever.

Jude 1:24-25

Circus performers who work on high wires often have a safety net below them. If they should stumble and fall the net keeps them from crashing to the floor and being hurt.

You have a safety net too. It's God. He protects you by cushioning your falls – yes, you'll still fall, He doesn't stop that – but He doesn't let the fall seriously hurt you. He wants you to learn from your stumbles, but not to give up because of them.

ChallengePoint

Wow! God loves you a lot! Just think about Him grabbing you when it seems you're going to fall on your face and then setting you back on your feet. He will protect you all the way into His presence in heaven.

God said, "Let us make human beings in Our image, to be like Ourselves."

Genesis 1:26

God took a pile of dirt and made it into the first man by breathing life into him. That's amazing and a gigantic miracle.

But even more amazing is that the first man was made in God's image. That man could do things God could do – think, feel, love, make decisions. You are like that first man. You are made in God's image.

ChallengePoint

God planned it that the people He created would be like Him. That's why people partner with Him in His work on this planet. You are like God and that mean's you're like Christ. Quite a responsibility, eh?

Giving

"Do to others whatever you would like them to do to you."
Matthew 7:12

"You get what you give" is another way to say this verse. If you treat others with kindness and respect, you are more likely to get that kind of treatment back. If you treat others with mean words and bad attitudes ... guess what ... you'll probably get that back.

God's wish, of course, is that you will show love and kindness to others and will share what He has given you with everyone you meet.

ChallengePoint

This is often called The Golden Rule. It's a foundational statement for how to treat others. But don't just be kind only so others will be kind back. That's a good starting point, but make every effort to be kind so that others will be able to see what God is like by how you live your life.

Trusting Him

In times of trouble, God is with us, and when we are knocked down, we get up again.

2 Corinthians 4:9

A boxer gets in the ring with the world champion. When the fight starts the rookie gets knocked down over and over. He keeps getting up and charging his opponent again. Would you do that? Sometimes when problems keep smacking you in the face, it's tempting to just fall down and play dead. Maybe the problems will stop if you stay down.

Why don't you? Because you know God is there helping you. He lifts you up, brushes the dust off your knees and helps you to keep on going.

ChallengePoint

You can trust God to help you every time you need help. He is always there. Sometimes you don't know He is there – you can't sense His presence until you actually need His help. Then, BOOM, there He is!

Knowing God by

His Love

Jesus wept.

John 11:35

A person doesn't cry over something he doesn't care about. There are a couple of times recorded in the Bible when Jesus cried. If He didn't care, He wouldn't cry.

Here's the formula:

- Jesus loves.
- He sees people hurting.
- He cries.

ChallengePoint

It's amazing to think about God feeling pain or sadness because of you, isn't it? But He loves you. When you love someone, you care about his pain. Remember how much God loves you – thank Him for His love!

Knowing God by

Being Thankful

December 31

Let your lives be built on Him. Then you will overflow with thankfulness.

Colossians 2:7

You know what an overflow looks like – when you're pouring a glass of milk but you get distracted by something on TV and the milk fills the glass and then runs all over the table and onto the floor. Yeah, that kind of overflow is a mess.

This verse is talking about a good overflow – when you get so filled up with all the wonderful, amazing things God has done for you that the thankfulness just flows over and runs into all parts of your life!

ChallengePoint

This is so cool. Have you ever been this thankful? Have you ever felt so blown away by God's awesome, wonderful, giving love that you can't even find words to express it? Think about all He does for you right now – and let the thanksgiving flow!

About the Author

Carolyn Larsen is an author, actress, and an experienced speaker with a God-given passion for ministering to women and children. She has spoken at conferences and retreats around the United States, Canada, and India. Carolyn has written over 40 books for children and adults. Her writing has won various awards. Carolyn lives in Glen Ellyn, Illinois, with her husband, Eric. They have three children and are proud grandparents.

Words of Jesus for Guys

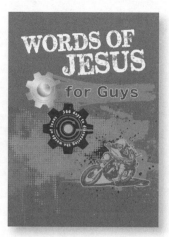

ISBN 978-1-4321-0132-9

E-ISBN 978-1-4321-0503-7

Words of Jesus for Guys is a 366-day devotional written especially for 8-12-year-olds. Each day features a Scripture verse, a lesson for the day, and a "Living It" section for practical application.

This funky and fresh devotional is sure to bring young readers closer to Jesus through His words on topics such as caring, sharing, and living a life that is pleasing to Him. Since children are confronted by tough decisions more and more every day, *Words of Jesus for Guys* will help them to make sense of it all by listening to what Jesus has to say. They will learn to answer their calling to shine their light for Him and live by His words.

The Bible in 366 Days for Guys

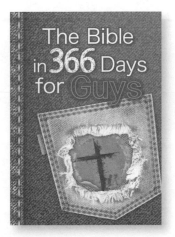

ISBN 978-1-4321-0061-2

E-ISBN 978-1-4321-0924-0

The devotions in *The Bible in 366 Days for Guys* have been especially written by Carolyn Larsen for boys aged 8 to 12. The 366 key Scripture passages from the Bible are accompanied by a short, yet powerful message for each day to reinforce what they learned.

Young readers can walk through the Bible from Genesis to Revelation and realize that God's Word has a special message for them each day.